KEN MILES

DAVE FRIEDMAN

THE SHELBY AMERICAN YEARS

CarTech®

CarTech®

CarTech®, Inc.
6118 Main Street
North Branch, MN 55056
Phone: 651-277-1200 or 800-551-4754
Fax: 651-277-1203
www.cartechbooks.com

Edit by Wes Eisenschenk
Layout by Connie DeFlorin

ISBN 978-1-61325-597-1
Item No. CT679

Library of Congress Cataloging-in-Publication Data

Names: Friedman, Dave, photographer.
Title: Ken Miles : the Shelby American years / David Friedman.
Description: Forest Lake, Minnesota : CarTech, [2021]
Identifiers: LCCN 2021058718 | ISBN 9781613255971 (Hardcover)
Subjects: LCSH: Miles, Ken, 1918-1966. | Shelby American, Inc.--History. | Automobile racing drivers--Great Britain--Biography. | Automobiles, Racing--United States--History--20th century. | Cobra automobile--History. | Ford GT40 automobile--History.
Classification: LCC GV1032.M437 F75 2021 | DDC 796.72092 [B]--dc23
LC record available at https://lccn.loc.gov/2021058718

Written, edited, and designed in the U.S.A.
Printed in China
10 9 8 7 6 5 4 3 2

Front cover: Ken Miles and Carroll Shelby hold the trophy for winning the Watkins Glen USRRC race in late June 1963. This image shows the real love that these two had for each other. If this photo looks familiar, it was the final image shown in the *Ford v Ferrari* movie.

DISTRIBUTION BY:

Europe
PGUK
63 Hatton Garden
London EC1N 8LE, England
Phone: 020 7061 1980 • Fax: 020 7242 3725
www.pguk.co.uk

Australia
Renniks Publications Ltd.
3/37-39 Green Street
Banksmeadow, NSW 2109, Australia
Phone: 2 9695 7055 • Fax: 2 9695 7355
www.renniks.com

Canada
Login Canada
300 Saulteaux Crescent
Winnipeg, MB, R3J 3T2 Canada
Phone: 800 665 1148 • Fax: 800 665 0103
www.lb.ca

TABLE OF CONTENTS

ACKNOWLEDGMENTS

I can never thank Carroll Shelby enough for the opportunity and friendship that he gave me during our time together. He believed enough in me and gave me my start, and I never looked back.

To all of my wonderful teammates in Venice who provided so many great first-person interviews over the years. Sadly, many are now gone, but their words will live forever.

To Wes Eisenschenk of Car Tech for believing in me and pushing me in the right direction.

To my great longtime friends Charlie Agapiou and Peter Miles for writing their forewords, which are beautiful and from their hearts.

Skye Schmidt helped with the all-important photo restoration.

My deepest thanks to my wife, Susan, who puts up with my artistic ways and offers incredible motivation.

FOREWORD BY PETER MILES AND CHARLIE AGAPIOU

My father was a pretty intense man. Everything he did was with full concentration and effort. He held the view that if something is worth doing, it is worth doing properly, and his mind was always going. He had a wide range of interests from classical music to gardening and was constantly working on improving our home life. He added on to the house, dug his own wine cellar in the hillside, and developed elaborate landscaping. I was expected to help.

I had no notion that my father was anything more than a typical father, until my teen years, when we held a dinner party for the British consul general as well as when the actor Steve McQueen came to the house to discuss a project and other things of interest.

At that time, our father-and-son relationship began to evolve into a friendship. As I look back on it, I find it a great pity that I never had the opportunity to know him from an adult point of view. Even now at nearly 70 years of age, I love to hear stories about my father to learn what he was really like. It's a feeling that I'm sure many people have when they've lost a parent while young. However, you have a choice: be mournful about it or review it in a more positive light with the realization that it's a part of this wonderful thing called life. I choose the latter.

Peter Miles

Dave Friedman is a renowned photographer. We met in the 1960s at Shelby American, where he was the official team photographer for the organization. He would be at the workshop and at the racetracks—always with camera in hand to document for Carroll Shelby what has become one of the most grand and unique periods in motor racing history. Dave's outstanding images from those years have captivated many people and happily supplied me with a permanent record of a very special time in my life.

Ken Miles was my hero.

When I was 19, I came to Hollywood and saw a sign in the window that said, "Mechanic Wanted." I was hired, and I had no idea how this job and my boss, Ken Miles, would impact my life in the most incredible way.

Ken always loved motor racing. He introduced me to this great sport, and I learned so much from him. We shared many good times together at the track. He was extremely competitive behind the wheel and a brilliant, hands-on race car engineer. Soon, Ken moved on to the position of competition manager at Shelby American, which left me without a job. He called me a few weeks later and asked if I wanted to join him at Shelby American, which was a very memorable journey for me.

I began working at Shelby American as part of the crew and then became Ken's crew chief, which was an amazing experience from start to finish. I am thrilled to see 50-plus years later that this extraordinary man is being recognized for his contributions to motor racing, and I believe the record should be set straight that he really did win Le Mans in 1966!

Ken will always be in my thoughts, and I miss him. I am very happy to have his son's (Peter's) friendship, and we always enjoy our conversations about his dad.

As I write this foreword, I want to thank Dave [Friedman] for his lifelong friendship and for writing this book about our friend Ken Miles.

Charlie Agapiou
Shelby American 1963–1967

I found this special image by mistake while looking for something else. It's the only image I have ever seen with Ken, young Peter, and a teenage Charlie Agapiou (far right) together. It was taken before the start of the Los Angeles Times Grand Prix at Riverside International Raceway in October 1962.

PREFACE

When Carroll Shelby asked me to record the memories of as many of the former Venice employees as I could contact, I took him up on his challenge. That was 25 years ago, and Carroll's suggestion resulted in many great first-person interviews with many old friends, many of whom are sadly gone now. Their interviews and great memories resulted in my very popular book *Remembering the Shelby Years: 1962–1969*.

During our weekly homemade chili lunch meetings, Carroll also asked me to write a book for him about his good friend Ken Miles. I told him that I would love to do so but the time wasn't right and the book would not sell. Well, Carroll, the time is finally right, so here we go, and I hope this is what you wanted.

Dave Friedman
Shelby American Photographer 1962–1965

1963 THE BEGINNING

I first met Ken Miles in 1958 when he was driving a Porsche 550RS for Otto Zipper's Precision Motor Cars in Beverly Hills, California. Ken always made time to talk to everyone, including a young upstart photographer named Dave. As time went by, Ken introduced me to his longtime sponsor, Otto Zipper, which became one of my first and best longtime clients.

Carroll Shelby Enterprises (later known as Shelby American) moved into Lance Reventlow's old shop at 1042 Princeton Dr. in Venice (a neighborhood in Los Angeles, California) around June 1962. In the beginning, the production and race shops were both in one location, and everyone worked on everything.

The first race car was built there, and it was scheduled to debut at the Los Angeles Times Grand Prix support race, the three-hour enduro for GT cars in October 1962. Bill Krause was signed as the first factory driver and debuted the car in spectacular fashion. He led the race by a half mile until a wheel hub broke, but the handwriting was on the wall.

Facing page: One of my earliest images of Ken Miles was taken at the Los Angeles Examiner Grand Prix in April 1959. Driving the Precision Motor Cars Porsche 550RS at Pomona Fairgrounds, Ken won this race overall against stellar competition.

In the fall of 1962, the small shop in Venice (a neighborhood in Los Angeles, California) was a one-building operation that housed the racing and production operations. Our first team car is under construction in the foreground. Legendary Shelby American crewmembers George Boskoff and Phil Remington appear in the foreground. These guys could do anything.

Original Shelby American team driver Bill Krause receives last-minute instruction from Carroll Shelby before practicing at Riverside in October 1962.

Bill Krause approaches Riverside's famed Turn 6 during the team's first race. The "XP" on the car door stood for experimental production. The organizers formed this special class so that the Cobra and new Corvette Z06 could run in the three-hour production enduro race. The Cobra did not finish due to a broken wheel hub, but it certainly foreshadowed things to come while it ran.

Dave MacDonald was the other top driver to join the team in February 1963.

February 1963

Ken came to Shelby American along with Dave MacDonald in February 1963. Shelby American was a young upstart company, and many people, including the motoring press, laughed at the company and many of its ideas. However, they didn't laugh for long because Ken helped put the company on the map in a short period of time.

Ken quickly inherited a few nicknames and became known to those around him as *Teddy Tea Bagger*, the *Hawk*, or *Sammy Side Bite*. Somewhat later, he added a new name to the list, *Teddy Tree Bagger*, after his famous encounter with the only tree on the Sebring circuit in 1964.

At that time, both Ken and MacDonald had made huge impact on the West Coast's very competitive and popular Sports Car Club of America (SCCA) and Cal Club sports car racing series. Both men had been involved in some of the most exciting, no-holds-barred racing during the 1962 season. By the time they came to Shelby American, both were crowd favorites wherever they appeared.

Ken brought his longtime mechanic Charlie Agapiou with him when he came to work for Shelby American.

"When Ken went to work for Shelby in February 1963, he asked me to go with him," Charlie said. "I started there as a general mechanic, and I was kind of a donkey in the beginning, doing whatever needed to be done."

Ken Miles was one of two top West Coast drivers who joined the Shelby American team in February 1963 after Bill Krause left to pursue other opportunities.

In 1962, Miles and MacDonald were responsible for some of the most exciting racing that was ever seen on the West Coast. Here, Miles, driving the Precision Motor Cars Ferrari 250 SWB (50) leads MacDonald's Don Steves Corvette (00) at Riverside International Raceway in June 1962.

It was always this close between these two great drivers, and the crowds loved it and came by the thousands to see it. This photo was taken at the Pomona Fairgrounds in July 1962.

Ken Miles was never beaten while driving this beautiful Ferrari 250 SWB for Otto Zipper. This photo was taken at Laguna Seca Raceway in October 1962.

Competition Manager

When Ken arrived at Shelby American's Venice shop in February 1963, he brought an air of professionalism, and it quickly rubbed off on the younger members of the crew—which was most of them. One of Ken's first ideas was to assign a crew chief and two mechanics to each the team's cars, and it stayed that way all season for the most part.

In addition to Charlie, Ken hired John Collins, who was another great

addition, to the Venice shop. John always said that Ken hired him because they were both British. They became good friends and stayed so until the end, when Ken died in August 1966.

"Ken was bloody quick and fiercely competitive in those Cobras (as he was in everything he drove), and he, MacDonald, and Bob Holbert became our first group of factory drivers in 1963," Charlie Agapiou said. "Ken did so well with Shelby's company that he became the company's real competition manager in 1963. We had a lot of great cars in our shop in 1963, and I worked on them all."

The first race for our first two-team cars was scheduled for February 2, 1963, at Riverside International Raceway. As was the custom in SCCA racing at that time, most drivers participated in multiple races, and Ken also drove Otto Zipper's Porsche RS61.

RIVERSIDE

FEB. 2 & 3

At Riverside International Raceway in early 1963, this was the program for the first race that featured both Ken and Mac-Donald in Shelby Cobras.

During this era of sports car racing, drivers often raced in several classes during the weekend. Here, MacDonald's Shelby Cobra (198) leads Ken's Porsche RS61 (50) during early-morning practice.

The Cobras ran away with their class, posting first- (MacDonald) and second-place (Miles) finishes in the production A&B race, which was heavily populated with Sting Rays. Ken also pulled down second in his Modified class with the Porsche RS61.

Paul Reinhart, the driver of a top Corvette, was asked by Hugh Randolph of the *Oakland Tribune* if the Cobras were that much faster.

"Fast?" he responded. "Man, that's the quickest thing I've ever seen on wheels. It's fast enough to win any Modified race. In the first lap, I could just barely keep MacDonald in sight. After that it was, 'Bye Bye Baby.' If Fangio had been in my Sting Ray, he wouldn't have come any closer."

As a side note, this was the last race for the 260-ci-powered Cobra.

Ken (98) leads Paul Reinhart's Z06 Corvette (6) and MacDonald (198) early in the A, B Production race.

Ken was always standing on the gas. This was the last race for the 260-ci-powered Shelby Cobra.

Ken drives the 260 Cobra. This was the only win for that particular car. In early March 1963, Ken took second place after teammate MacDonald at Riverside International Raceway.

Ken (98) and MacDonald (198) were the best of friends and worked well together in the shop, but on the track, they were fierce rivals, and the crowds loved it. Here, at Riverside International Raceway, the Sting Rays had no chance. For the Cobras, many more wins would come in the future.

Ken also drove Otto Zipper's Precision Motor Cars Porsche RS61 during the Modified race that weekend. Zipper was a longtime sponsor of Ken's racing activities and a close friend.

289 Cobra – Dodger Stadium

The first race for the legendary 289-ci-powered Cobra was in the Dodger Stadium parking lot on March 2, 1963, as a crowd of 18,000 looked on during the two-day event. Again, Ken drove the Porsche to victory in the 15-lap, Modified class event. Both classes were loaded with talent. MacDonald placed ahead of Ken by 2 seconds in the Sunday cofeature.

Ken, in the Shelby Cobra (298), leads Bob Bondurant in the Washburn Chevrolet Corvette Z06 (614). This was the first race for the legendary 289-ci-powered Cobra, and the two Shelby American entries ran first and second both days.

Ken practices in the parking lot of beautiful Dodger Stadium for the race weekend that was staged there on March 2 and 3, 1963.

Outside of the press conference are (left to right) Skip Hudson (note the cast on his right foot), Ken Miles, Peter Jopp (seated in Cobra), Lew Spencer, Dave MacDonald, and Carroll Shelby.

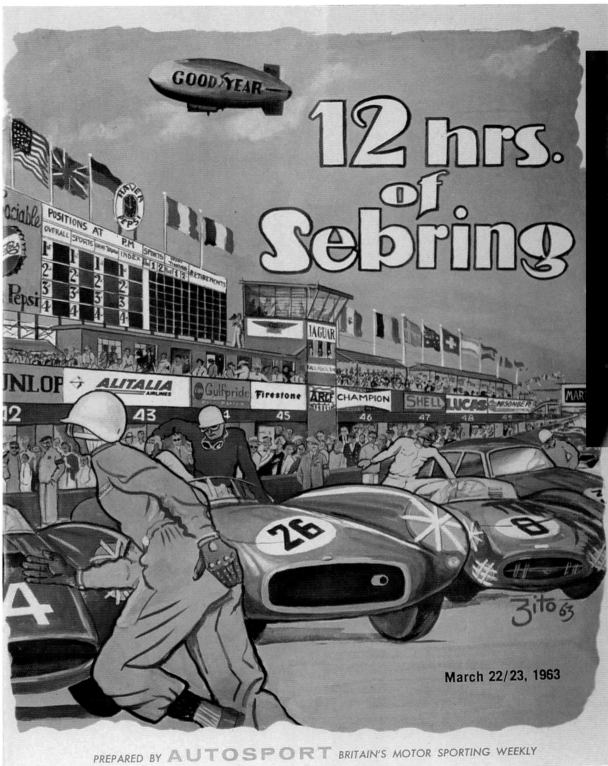

Ken is deep in thought before practice begins.

This was the program for the March 24, 1963, 12 Hours of Sebring.

Practice makes for perfect, and the Shelby crew was one of the best when it came to making pit stops. The crew is seen practicing on the Ken Miles/Lew Spencer entry.

As a crewman works on the oil pan, Ken inspects the underside of the engine on the hoist. Otto Zipper, a longtime Miles sponsor, looks on.

The Shelby crew pushes the Miles/ Spencer entry toward the starting grid. Lew Spencer, right rear, wears his team Cobra jacket.

Carroll Shelby holds a last-minute drivers' meeting. In the back row (left to right) are Ken Miles, Ed Leslie, and Carroll Shelby, In the front row (left to right) are Phil Hill and Dave MacDonald.

Ken Miles (16) leads the Ferrari GTO driven by Charlie Hayes (32) out of the Webster Turns early in the race.

Ken is a picture of poise and concentration.

Parked at the side of the course, Ken looks for gremlins under the hood. He found plenty with the steering and the car was designated as a DNF (did not finish) early in the race.

The No. 12 Cobra comes in for a night pit stop. Ken and Lew Spencer took over this ride after their car expired early in the race. Spencer sits in the car while Ken (right foreground) prepares to relieve him. Carroll Shelby (right rear), in a team jacket, walks away. This car finished 11th overall and was the only Shelby Cobra to finish.

At the awards ceremony, Carroll Shelby speaks while Alex Ulmann (far left), Lew Spencer, Phil Hill (hidden behind Shelby), and Ken stand on the podium. Although the car finished in 11th place, they still won the GTO class.

Back in California

The Shelby Cobra team did not participate in the first two United States Road Racing Championship (USRRC) races at Daytona or Pensacola in the series' first year of 1963. However, Ken teamed with Holbert in Holbert's Porsche 718 RS61 to win the overall at Pensacola.

Laguna Seca Championship Road Races

The full Shelby team, with its three cars, first appeared at the Laguna Seca round in June 1963. This was a race where both classes, the Manufacturers and the Drivers, were run together, so the Cobras were never in contention for the overall win. Ken followed his team orders and ran second behind Holbert until he had to pit to repair a shifting problem late in the race. Ken finished ninth overall and five laps behind the leader.

Ken Miles drove a Sunbeam Alpine in one of the support races at the June 1963 Laguna Seca United States Road Racing Championship (USRRC) race weekend. Note the name of Ken's then-closed shop on the side of the car. Charlie Agapiou worked there and said, "I started working for Ken in 1962, when he had his own shop in Hollywood. We were running Sunbeam Alpines in the club races, and I was taking care of them along with Jean Stucki. Ken was always in trouble financially, and one day when we came to work, the bloody Feds had locked the place up."

Ken Miles (50) leads Ron Dale's Porsche Speedster (163) down the front straight.

Carroll (far left) conducts a small drivers meeting as MacDonald (back to the camera), Ken (far right), and Bob Holbert listen to the instructions. Holbert joined the team in March 1963.

Ken Miles (198) leads the Ed Cantrell's Ferrari GTO (11) at Laguna Seca.

Ken's Shelby Cobra (198) leads Don Devine's Scarab (26) and Stan Peterson's Ferrari GTO Berlinetta (7) at the top of Laguna Seca's famed Corkscrew.

Following team orders, Bob Holbert leads Ken Miles through Turn Nine.

Shelby and his crew show the pit board to Ken (198) from the pits at Laguna Seca.

Ken makes a quick pit stop to tell the crew that he is having a shifting problem. Jerry Titus's Genie-Corvair (16) can be seen on track behind Ken.

Ken makes a quick pit stop to have the crew replace a cotter key in his shift linkage. He was back out in matter of seconds and still finished ninth overall and fourth in the Manufacturers' Division.

Watkins Glen

The next USRRC race was at Watkins Glen International on June 30 in Upstate New York. That is where I took the famous photo of Shelby and Ken in the winner's circle that appeared as the last image seen in the *Ford v Ferrari* film.

Ken finished second in the GT class, and Shelby let him run in the Drivers' race too. Ken's crew quickly changed tires and filled his car with fuel. Ken managed to finish third, a lap behind Holbert, his Shelby teammate, who drove the Porsche RS61. Holbert praised Ken after the race, telling the *Star-Gazette*, "I don't know how he did it. He's really strong to drive two races in a day with a Cobra."

Ken and Carroll Shelby hold the trophy for winning the Watkins Glen USRRC race in late June 1963. This image shows the real love that these two had for each other. If this photo looks familiar, it was the final image shown in the *Ford v Ferrari* movie.

Lake Garnett Grand Prix

On their way back West, the Shelby Cobras were entered in the Lake Garnett Grand Prix on July 6 and 7 in Garnett, Kansas. About 65,000 spectators surrounded the lake and watched Bob Johnson, MacDonald, and Ken sweep the podium in the A, B, C production race.

Ken's car was then entered in the Modified feature race, which he won by dispatching the field, which inlcuded Chevrolet's top mount, a Grand Sport Corvette.

A mock gravestone was created in the infield by Shelby Racing Manager and Competition Director Al Dowd and crew members with the headstone reading: "Here Lies the Corvettes."

Spectators watch Shelby American Inc. pull into the Lake Garnett paddock as Shelby American prepares to unload its den of snakes. (Herb Williams Photos Courtesy of Tracy Modlin)

Carroll Shelby, Ken, and Jim
Cullenton (left to right) stand at
the back of Dave MacDonald's
Cobra. (Herb Williams Photos
Courtesy of Tracy Modlin)

Ken smiles at *Road & Track*
Photographer Herb Williams
at Lake Garnett. (Herb Williams
Photos Courtesy of Tracy Modlin)

Carroll is presented the checkered flag by Chief Starter Dale Duncan while Ken cools off with a cup of water. Claude C. Anderson, a Ford dealership owner in Garnett, Kansas, stands by in the checkered shirt. (Herb Williams Photos Courtesy of Tracy Modlin)

Pomona Fairgrounds

Ken drove Otto Zipper's Dolphin-Porsche in the Modified race at Pomona Fairgrounds on July 13, 1963. In a very close race, he was beaten by Dave MacDonald (driving his factory Cobra) at the finish line.

In mid-July 1963, Ken (50) drove the Precision Motor Cars Dolphin-Porsche in the very popular Pomona Fairgrounds Classic Sports Car Club (CSCC) race weekend. He battled his Shelby American teammate and good friend Dave MacDonald (barely visible in back) all weekend but to no avail.

MacDonald leads Ken in the Modified race and went on to win both days. Ken finished second.

USRRC Kent

The following USRRC race was at Kent, Washington, on July 20 and 21. For some strange reason, there was no continuity to the series calendar, and the teams had to bounce back and forth across the country constantly.

There was a change in Shelby's game plan, however, and the Cobras were to run in numerical (97, 98, and 99) order, and that's exactly what they did for the entire race, even finishing first, second, and third in the final standings.

Permission was granted for all three cars to run in the Drivers' race as well. Once again, the crews quickly changed the tires and topped off the fuel. And, away they went. Ken earned a hard-fought fifth-place finish in that race.

The Cobra team was at its best when running together in numerical order. Holbert (99) leads Ken (98) and MacDonald (97) at the Kent, Washington, USRRC event in late July 1963. The Shelby team really found its mojo by then and never let up.

General description of car: (specifying materials of bodywork)

Open roadster with aluminum coachwork over steel tube body. Frame manufactured by A.C. Cars, Ltd. (England), 2 passenger, Girling disc brakes standard equipment. Car supplied with or without metal or fiberglass hardtop or with canvas foldingtop. Also aerodynamic hardtop coupe.

Photographs to be affixed below:

 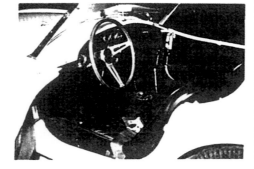

 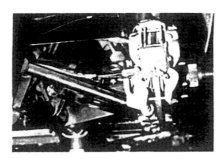

I became friends with Ken while spending many long evenings in his office pasting up these dreadful homologation papers. We had many long chats, and he once told me that he would "rather be killed in a race car than be eaten up by cancer." I've never forgotten that.

Goodwood

Ken's next attempt to race in a Cobra was at an event where he wasn't wanted in the first place. It was the Royal Automotive Club (RAC) Tourist Trophy race, which was being run on the weekend of August 24 that year at the Goodwood Circuit in the United Kingdom. The John Ailment Racing Team was to run its first race with its new Shelby Cobras. Ailment wanted Jack Sears and Bob Olthoff as drivers, but Sears was unavailable for this race, so Shelby told Ailment to use Miles.

A serious problem happened at scrutineering (tech inspection) due to an interpretation of the homologation rules regarding the wheels. The RAC disallowed the same wheels that the cars ran at Le Mans in June 1963. A huge row that almost became a fistfight occurred, but the cars were not allowed to run.

"This whole incident was a real comedy of errors," Ken said.

Facing Page: Ken watches from the foreground as a frantic argument takes place over the homologation of Cobra's wheels at the Royal Automotive Club (RAC) Tourist Trophy race at Goodwood, United Kingdom, in August 1963. The decision to disqualify both Cobras led to a serious encounter with the team owner John Willment, and a fistfight nearly ensued. Jeff Uren remembered, "Our first race with the Cobras was at the Goodwood TT in August 1963. We had Ken Miles from Shelby American and Bob Oltoff as drivers, but we didn't get through scrutineering because of homologation problems. It was not a very spectacular start to our racing program. We had wanted another driver, but he was busy, and Ken Miles was put upon us (in a matter of speaking) by the Shelby organization."

Santa Barbara

Labor Day weekend had Ken back in the Dolphin-Porsche, where he started near the back of the field. By the fourth lap, he moved all the way up to third place, but the rear axle let go.

"And the car was finally running right," said a dejected Ken.

Road America

By the time that the Road America 500 rolled around in September, the Cobras had been made to be extremely reliable, but they had yet to prove themselves in the long-distance event. For this 500-mile race, Ken and Holbert were teamed together. Ken qualified for the pole position in a

By September 1963, the competition knew that when this truck showed up in the paddock area, they were in for a very long day.

Ken runs away from the starting field early in the race during the beautiful Road America 500 in September 1963.

large starting field of 61 entries that mixed Modified and GT cars together.

As the green flag fell, Ken and Holbert ran in the top five for most of the race. Near the halfway point of the race, Ken was called in for a brake puck change and had to go like hell to catch up to the leaders. Near the end of the race, Ken's car began to smoke as he crossed the finish line. The engine blew. Ken and Holbert finished second overall and first in the GT category, finally finishing a long-distance race for Shelby American.

Carroll tells Ken to pit for gas the old-fashioned way (by pit board). Radios weren't used at that time.

Ken took a few laps in the 99 car to solve a handling problem.
Here, he enters the pits with Carroll Shelby on the pit board.

Ken sits on the starting grid for the Road America 500 in September 1963. Among those attending the car are Louie Unser, Ole Olsen, and Red Pierce.

Ken pits for fuel and tires. Jim Culleton checks the brakes while Ole Olsen fuels the car. Ken exits the car at the rear (dark helmet) while Bob Holbert (white helmet) on the far left prepares to enter the car for his stint.

As Carroll Shelby and driver Lew Spencer operate the quick jack, Ken, far left, has a look at the front end.

Bridgehampton

Next was the Bridgehampton 500 on a very chilly September day in Long Island, New York. Being a Fédération Internationale de l'Automobile (FIA) points race and another 500-mile race that took place only a week after Road America, a lot of work needed to be done.

At a local Ford dealership, engines were changed, brakes were rebuilt, and new tires were mounted. On race day, Ken started in pole position; Gurney and Holbert filled out the front row. Running to team orders, Gurney won, and Miles finished second; Holbert didn't finish. This was Shelby American's first FIA win. The Cobras were finally proving to be reliable for long-distance racing.

A very strong Shelby team sits in the starting grid at Bridgehampton. Bob Holbert is in the foreground, Dan Gurney is in the middle, and Ken Miles is in the background.

Facing Page: Bob Holbert (left) and Ken are in victory lane for the Road America 500. The team finished second overall and first in the GT class. This was the Shelby team's first win in a long-distance race.

Ken scrapes a bug off Dan Gurney's windshield on the stating grid of the September 1963 Bridgehampton 500.

Bob Holbert (97), Dan Gurney (99), and Ken Miles (98) are ready for the start of the race. Behind them are the two lightweight Jaguar XKEs of the Cunningham team.

Intensity gets the job done, and Ken was always intense during the race.

As Carroll Shelby (holding the stopwatch) waits for the cars to appear, Red Pierce brings out Ken's final pit sign. Ken finished second to winner Dan Gurney. It was the Shelby American team's first FIA race win.

Mid-Ohio

Next was the USRRC finale on September 22, 1963, at the Mid-Ohio circuit. Ken finished second in the Manufacturers' race and won the Drivers' race. In the final Drivers' race standings, Ken finished second, and the Shelby American team won the Manufacturers' trophy.

Canadian Sports Car Grand Prix

Ken was sent to the Mosport circuit in Canada for the Canadian Sports Car Grand Prix. He finished second, driving one of the white Ford of Canada's Comstock Racing Team Cobras while the rest of the team returned to

Venice to prepare for the Los Angeles Times Grand Prix in October.

After the Mosport circuit, Ken returned to Venice to resume his competition manager duties and prepare the team for the annual West Coast Fall Pro Series. There was a lot of testing and Cooper modifications to be done, and there was not much time to do it. Ken did not drive in the Fall Series but wore his manager's hat well. Jack Hoare remembered it in detail.

"I was working for Team Meridian and Skip Hudson at the Times GP in 1963 when Ken Miles came to our pit and asked me to come and see him at the Shelby pit when I had a break," Hoare said. "So, I did, and he offered me a job.

Ken drove one race in Ford of Canada's famous white Cobra. This was at Mosport Park in Ontario, Canada, on September 28, 1963. He finished second in the GT class.

Ken loved the kids and always
spent plenty of time with them.

"When I showed up at the Venice shop, Ken asked me
what I wanted to do, and I told him that I wanted to work
in the engine shop. At that point, he took me back to
meet the head of the engine shop, Cecil Bowman. There
was no question in my mind that Ken was the man who
ran that shop."

After the series finished, Ken, MacDonald, and Shelby
were presented with brand-new 1964 Thunderbirds to
drive. This presentation took place at Culver City Ford,
which was not far from our shop.

Ken Miles warms up Dave
MacDonald's King Cobra
as Craig Lang pushes the
car in the pits at Riverside in
October 1963.

At the end of the 1963 season, Ken, Dave MacDonald and
Carroll Shelby were given 1964 Thunderbirds to drive at a
ceremony at Culver City Ford.

Hawaiian Grand Prix

Team Shelby loaded its race cars and sent them to Hawaii for the Hawaiian Grand Prix. Ken and Craig Lang made the voyage with crew chiefs Wally Peat and Al Dowd in tow, landing at Honolulu International Airport via a Pan American carrier on October 24. MacDonald had arrived two days prior.

MacDonald started in pole position in his Cobra for the A, B, C, D Production race with Ken (Cobra) flanked to his right in P2 in the five-lap prelims. Ken captured the win in the short event, as MacDonald was hobbled by a blown tire. Lang won the Modified prelim in the Cooper Cobra.

Sunday's Hawaiian Grand Prix, which was shortened from 50 to 26 laps, was all Cobra, as Lang got out to a quick lead with MacDonald overtaking him on Lap 5. MacDonald paced the next 22 circuits with the final 9 laps being a contentious back and forth between the two racers. Lang crossed the stripe first, and MacDonald and Ken crossed the finish nearly neck and neck, respectively, in second and third.

Brock Coupe

In late October 1963, the biggest project to ever be completed from the ground up was launched in Shelby American's Venice shop, and Ken was a big part of it from start to finish.

The Brock Coupe Project, as it was originally called, was officially launched, and it was a 24-hours-a day, 7-days-a-week, 365-days a year project. John Ohlsen, John Collins, and the crew were always in need of quick solutions, and the answers had to be immediate.

Since Ken and Phil Remington (Rem) were always there and Pete Brock was not, you could always turn to them for a positive response.

This was the first day of the Brock Coupe Project, as it was known at the time. In late October 1963, Pete Brock, (right) prepares to set the head room for the coming car as Ken sits in the chassis while Shelby watches and John Ohlsen (left) watches carefully. I remember this as if it were yesterday.

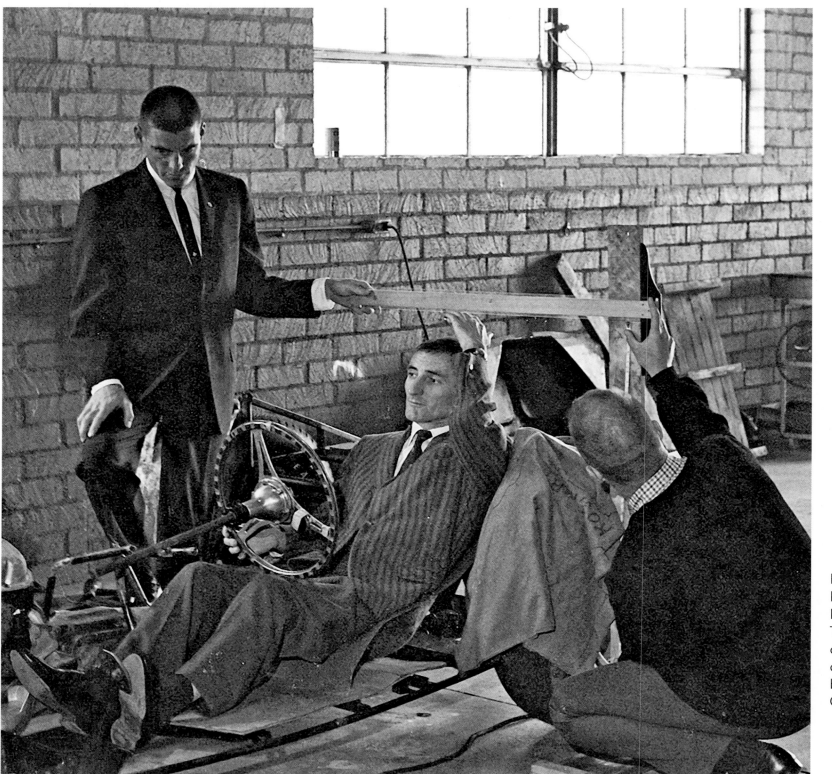

Pete measures Ken's headroom as MacDonald assists. The buck was built on the wrecked chassis of Skip Hudson's Daytona Cobra roadster.

"It always seemed to me that Ken was really the man in charge of the coupe project," said Bill Eaton. "He, Rem, and Donn Allen always had the answers. Pete was teaching at the school at Riverside with John Timanus and was seldom there."

Now, it was back to overseeing the coupe project for Ken, and time was of the essence because the car needed to be ready to test and be shipped to Daytona by early February 1964. Also, the 427 Cobra that was to be run at Sebring in 1964 was in the process of being built. That was literally a *what if* project dreamt up by Ken in a conversation with Shelby.

Ken makes his daily rounds of the Venice shop activities as John Collins, one of Ken's recent hires, works on the early stages of the coupe frame.

As the coupe project progresses, Ken, Pete Brock (standing left), and Phil Remington (standing right) check for wheel size. John Ohlsen is barely seen behind Remington.

Nassau Speed Week

Soon, it was off to Nassau for the annual Speed Week. Nassau was a well-known destination for the racing crowd, and it was always a well-attended year-end event that became better known more for its parties than its racing.

The Oakes Field racing circuit was a very rough old airport and always wreaked havoc with the suspension on the Shelby cars. This also happened to be the debut for the Chevrolet factory-backed Corvette Grand Sport, and try as they did, Shelby and Ken could glom no information from the tight-lipped drivers or crewmembers.

Ken's luck at Nassau was no better than the rest of the Shelby drivers, and they drew a big "did not finish" (DNF) for the entire time.

Upon returning to the Venice shop, Ken was saddled with overseeing the completion of the coupe project that he was to test at Riverside in mid- to late January 1964. The 427 Cobra also had to be completed so that it could be tested the same day. It was a real run to the roses.

The Shelby crew works on Ken's car, No. 98 (foreground), in the large hanger where all of the competitors were housed during Nassau Speed Week in December 1963.

Shelby tries to see under the hood of the new Corvette Grand Sport as Ken attempts to grill a tight-lipped Roger Penske about the car.

Ken enjoys some of the Nassau sun while standing in the pit area.

The Year of the Cobra

THE **SHELBY FORD COBRA THE CAR OF THE YEAR**, MAKES ITS FINAL RACING APPEARANCE OF THE YEAR DURING NASSAU SPEED WEEK DEC. 1-8TH IN THE BAHAMAS- IN ITS FIRST YEAR OF PRODUCTION THE CAR WON THE U.S. ROAD RACING CIRCUIT MFGR'S CHAMPIONSHIP WITH 111 POINTS TO 28 FOR FERRARI IN SECOND.. ..THE SCCA CLASS "A" PRODUCTION CROWN AND THE USRRC DRIVERS CHAMPIONSHIP.. WITH BOB HOLBERT IN FIRST AND KEN MILES' SECOND.

KEN MILES

BOB HOLBERT

Manning

THE SHELBY COOPER FORDS IN THE PRO-FALL CIRCUIT WON THE RIVERSIDE AND LAGUNA SECA GRAND PRIX AND THE SECOND BIGGEST POT IN KENT, WASH. GRAND PRIX.

A cartoon that appeared near the end of the season shows Ken Miles and Bob Holbert. It was truly the year of the Cobra, and it would only get better for the small company that was laughed at in the beginning. Shelby American had the last laugh.

Ken Miles (97) leads Mike Gammino's Ferrari GTO (23) on the rough Oaks Field Nassau circuit. That circuit was not kind to the Shelby American entries.

Back at Dodger Stadium

Ken wrapped up the calendar year back in the Porsche for Otto Zipper and Bob Estes and won the 15-lap Modified main event around the 11-turn course. It was a fitting end to an eventful season, as Ken's tasks at Shelby American would limit his moonlighting with other car owners.

NASCAR a Calling

Early in November, Ken's short-lived NASCAR career was launched. At the Golden State 400, Ken was invited to drive a factory 1963 Ford for the Holman-Moody Racing Team.

Since it was a true learning experience and an altogether new form of racing to him, Ken told me that the Stock Car was a very different animal compared to what he was used to driving. Those qualities showed during practice, as he rolled his Ford but climbed out with nary a scratch on his body.

A backup car was unloaded for the race, but Ken did not push his luck and stayed in a safe position. Even by doing that, he went on a few off-course excursions. By the race's end, he finished in 11th overall position, several laps back. And so ended Ken's NASCAR adventure.

Ken (right) talks to Skip Hudson (center) and Dan Gurney (left) at Riverside in November 1963.

Ken's weekly testing sessions at Riverside helped make the Cobra what it became.

John Ohlsen continues work on the coupe while Ken holds a meeting in his office in the background. Without Ohlsen, there would have been no competed coupe in time for Daytona in early February 1964.

Ted Sutton needed a shoehorn to get that 427-ci engine into a stock 289-ci Cobra chassis, but he did it. Soon after, Shelby and then Ken took some test laps around the neighborhood.

Ted Sutton (foreground) is hard at work on the first 427 Cobra. This was an interesting Ken Miles project, which was slated to run, hopefully, at Sebring in March 1964. Ken (dark sweater), Remington, and Brock discuss the progress of the Daytona coupe build.

The coupe nears its finish. It's hard to believe that this massive job was completed in just under 90 days in this tiny shop with so much else going on. Give thanks to John Ohlsen, Phil Remington, Ken, Pete Brock, and so many others who made it a reality.

Ken (light shirt) gives the car a quick look over before retiring to the truck for his morning tea.

It's test day at Riverside for the Daytona coupe and the 427 Cobra. Ken would drive the coupe and Bondurant would drive the 427. John Collins, John Ohlsen, and Dan Doniack of Shelby Goodyear are at the front of the coupe, while Jerry Bondio sits in the truck. Ken is probably having his morning tea.

Ken leaves the pits and heads toward Turn 1 as the coupe test gets underway.

After one lap, Ken goes flat-out past the Riverside pit area.

Ken proved that the Daytona coupe was for real that day. Ted Sutton said, "When we got back to the shop, Ken asked me to put the coupe on jack stands and pull the differential cover so we could count the teeth on the gear ratio. We had a stock rear end and the RPMs told us that we were going 15 to 20 mph faster than the roadsters did on the long Riverside straight." Pete's theory was proven right.

COBRA NEWS

DEKE HOULGATE—public relations
5478 wilshire blvd. · suite 208
los angeles 36, california, U.S.A.
telephone: (a. c. 213) 933-5904

ADVANCE FOR SATURDAY P.M. (Jan. 7, 1964)
SUNDAY A.M. (Jan. 8, 1964)

Carroll Shelby, who surprised the world twice with the Ford Cobra and the Cooper Ford, has another ace up the sleeve of his racing jacket.

Shelby confirmed reports this week that a 200-mile-an-hour version of the racing Cobra is being built in Los Angeles.

The new car is called the "Daytona Cobra" because it will probably be introduced there, Shelby said. It is a very radical aluminum-bodied coupe built on the AC chassis and powered by the Cobra version of the Ford Fairlane 289 cubic inch engine.

Shelby said the car will conform to F.I.A. regulations qualifying Gran Turismo (grand touring) cars for international manufacturers' point races.

The Daytona Cobra project is under the joint supervision of chief designer Pete Brock, chief engineer Phil Remington and racing director Ken Miles. Fabrication is being done under tight security at Shelby's plant in Venice, Calif.

Basically the car is designed to improve aerodynamics, Brock said. It won't look a bit like the Ford Cobra, he reported.

(more)

Page 2

"The nose is longer and looks more pointed. The overall height and center of gravity are lower. The tail is chopped, and the car has an underpan that sweeps up in the rear," Brock said.

"The configuration is different -- particularly back of the rear wheels -- from any contemporary GT racing car. You have to call this body shape a radical departure."

Another major innovation will be a movable vane in the rear that can be adjusted to the ideal aerodynamic setting. Other design features will include a lower seating position for the driver, stronger support for the car's body and structural changes to offset the stresses of tremendous "G loads" during high speed cornering.

The 200-mile-an-hour estimate has been offered by aerodynamicists who have examined Brock's designs. Initial testing will take place early this year.

The full-race Cobra now commonly attains speeds of 165 miles an hour despite what is regarded as a "giveaway" of 20 to 25 miles an hour in air drag to such sleek racers as the Ferrari GTO.

Designer Brock is the senior employee at Shelby American, Inc., in Venice, holding the title of Manager, Special Projects, although he is only 27 years old.

He went to work for Shelby nearly three years ago, helping to operate the School of High Performance Driving, Goodyear Racing Tire distributorship and the young automobile firm from its crude beginnings in Santa Fe Springs, Calif.

Before Brock moved to California he was employed for more than two years at General Motors in the "Special Vehicle Development" project. At the time the Corvette Stingray was on the drawing boards.

(more)

12 Hours of Sebring

Soon, it was time to return to Sebring International Raceway for the annual 12-hour race. By the time the cars were unloaded at the hanger, the 427 Cobra was actually looking like a real race car. The fenders had been widened to accept racing tires, and Ken and Remington had cut holes on the nose of the car to increase the cooling to the radiator.

Just before practice began, Shelby had a word with a few of his team drivers as was his custom. Not long after practice started, Ken managed to hit the only tree on the Sebring circuit, which caused significant damage to the front end and bent the car's frame.

Once back in the hanger, the damage was assessed. Ken felt the car could be repaired, but the crew was not so sure. The crew immediately went to work on what would be an exhausting all-nighter, and Ken was right in there among them. As the crew was finishing a very long night, an engine change was ordered.

After everything was done, the car looked reasonably race ready from a distance. Ken started well back in the field (49th place). He battled with A. J. Foyt (who drove the Mecom Corvette Grand Sport) for a number of laps and he worked his way to 46th place by the end of the first hour.

By the end of the second hour, Ken was up to 45th place and beginning to feel that brake problems were coming. By the end of the third hour, Ken moved up to 39th place, but he had to pit with overheating brakes. After

Before the start of practice at Sebring, Remington, Shelby, Ken, MacDonald, and John Holman have a pre-race discussion.

Facing Page: A meeting of the minds is seen during a pit stop during this Riverside testing session: (left to right) Pete Brock, Ken, Charlie Agapiou and John Collins. The Sunbeam Tiger (background) acted as my chase car while Pete's yarn tufts are seen taped to the coupe body.

Ken had driven the first 29 laps, he handed the problematic car over to John Morton.

Morton drove extremely well despite experiencing total brake loss and serious engine problems. Morton and Ken both had the fastest laps in the car (3:15.2), but the car was fatiguing by the minute. It was during Morton's driving stint on Lap 81 that the engine finally let go. So ended Ken's experiment with the first 427 Cobra. With his driving adventure over, Ken pitched in to help in the pits.

Toward the end of the race, Bob Johnson, who was in the highest running Cobra, was involved in a spectacular crash on the front straight, and we all thought that there was no way he could have survived. Ken was sent by Shelby to get a report from the medical unit, and he reported that somehow Johnson had survived with a concussion and a black eye.

Upon the return to our shop in Venice, the 427 Cobra and what was left of the Gurney/Johnson 289 Cobra were promptly cut up and thrown in the dumpster.

Last-minute cooling adjustments are performed by Remington as Ken and Al Dowd watch from left. Also seen are Shelby (wheelchair), Ray Geddes (suit), and Peyton Cramer (left rear).

After Ken hit the only tree on the Sebring circuit, a long night of frantic repairs was in order. Ken fires up the welding torch while John Morton stands by. Jeff Schoolfield (left) works on straightening the body.

Ken observes the well-battered front-end damage that included a bent frame.

Under the watchful eye of Ken Miles (far right), Phil Remington pounds out metalwork while John Morton welds and Jim Culleton and Gary Koike provide much-needed help. After an exhausting all-nighter, the car was somewhat drivable.

After starting near the rear of the 66-car field, Ken moved up swiftly to run in the middle of the pack. Here, he passes Donald Kearny's Triumph Spitfire (64).

Still showing the effects of the amazing all-night repair job, Ken does his best to keep the car going for as long as he can.

Early in the race, Ken Miles (1) leads the Corvette Grand Sport of A. J. Foyt (2). These two raced for many laps like this with multiple lead changes. Once finally complete, the Cobra didn't look too bad from a distance.

The damaged front end is visible as Ken rounds the famous Sebring Hairpin.

The Cobra 427 makes a pit stop to check for various problems.

John Morton did a
great job in relief of
Ken. Morton even
equaled Ken's fastest
lap time in the car at
3:15.2.

Ken is running
well in spite of
brake and engine
problems.

This is a pit stop for a brake pad change. The brakes on that car were completely stock, and they were pushed well beyond the limit. The crewman (left) is working on the brakes as Gary Koike (right) pours water on the overheated brakes, and Charlie Agapiou stands by to help. After 81 laps, the engine finally let go, and the car was scrapped upon its return to the shop.

When his car expired, Ken assumed his competition manager position. Here, he points out something to Jim Culleton during a tire change. Bob Bondurant sits in the car ready to go.

Shelby and Miles discuss the condition of Bob Johnson after his spectacular front-straight crash near the end of the race. Somehow, Johnson walked away with fairly minor injuries.

USRRC Pensacola

When we left Sebring, our next stop was the USRRC race in Pensacola, Florida, on April 5. As usual, Ken ran away from the small field in the Manufacturers' race. In the Drivers' race, Ken finally had his chance to drive one of the Shelby King Cobras.

Unfortunately, it was to no avail, as Ken had nothing but continuous mechanical problems and finally retired from the race after 61 of 74 laps.

FIA Phoenix

On April 19, Shelby American ran the FIA race at the new Phoenix International Raceway. As usual it was hot, but the new course was very nice and well laid out. Ken drove his trusty 289 Cobra in the GT race and, against a large field, ran away to an overwhelming win. In the 60-lap open, Ken brought his Cobra home in eighth place.

Ken races through the back part of the track as he
passes a Sunbeam Alpine.

Jerry Titus in the Cheetah (58) gave chase to Ken (15) late in the FIA race but left on Lap 23 with engine failure.

Ken takes the checkered flag for the Phoenix GT race.

Riverside USRRC

Once the USRRC series reached the West Coast, the fields became considerably larger, and the crowds increased significantly from the previous races.

At Riverside, the Manufacturers' race drew a field of 22 entries. Ken was the fast qualifier with teammate Ed Leslie in the second position. When the green flag fell, Ken took the immediate lead and never looked back. Ken also ran his Cobra in the Drivers' race and finished fourth overall against a very strong field. One moment that I have always treasured was Ken finding me on the track and smiling and waving at me.

At the Riverside USRRC race in April 1964, the Cobra fans turned out in droves.

I always expected to get my customary wave from Ken. This time, it was as he crested Riverside's Turn 7. I have never forgotten Ken's great sense of humor.

Monterey USRRC

At Laguna Seca on May 3, Ken qualified in second position for the Manufacturers' race. He got off to a good start but had two off-course excursions and finished the race in second place to teammate Ed Leslie with fellow Cobra stablemate Bob Johnson in third.

The beautiful Laguna Seca circuit was the site of the May 3, 1964, annual USRRC event run. Ken (50) and Ed Leslie (98) are already pulling away from the field at Turn 1. Giving chase are the Porsche 904s of Don Wester (60), Kurt Neumann (32), and Scooter Patrick (33), as well as Dick Guldstrand's Corvette (56), Bob Johnson's Shelby Cobra (33), and Merle Brennan's Jaguar E-Type Lightweight (66). Ken made a rare off-course excursion on Lap 4 and finished second to Leslie.

Pacific Northwest Grand Prix

A week later, at Kent, Washington, Ken regained his winning form, and that form carried through for most of the rest of the season. Ken also ran the Cobra in the Drivers' race and finished a strong fourth overall against a stellar field.

Ken is in the lead during the USSRC Manufacturers' race at Kent, Washington.

Charlie gives Ken a pit signal at Kent. Were two people ever more on the same wavelength as these two?

Dave MacDonald

When Dave MacDonald came to us at Shelby American in February 1963, he was already well known as a hugely popular, successful, and spectacular West Coast Corvette driver, whose talent was instantly recognizable. MacDonald was a quiet and unassuming man except when he was on the race-track, and we all loved him.

I first met MacDonald in February 1960 and immediately became lifelong friends with him, his beautiful wife, Sherry, and their two young children, Rich and Vicki.

MacDonald's contributions to the early Shelby American team were huge and numerous. He was one of our mainstays and was an irreplaceable member of our team. When MacDonald was killed at Indianapolis on May 30, 1964, a real dose of reality set in at our small Venice shop. The day of his funeral was the day the Snake cried.

Dave MacDonald sits in the cockpit of the very fast Lang Cooper at Laguna Seca in April 1964. He is surrounded by Crew Chief Wally Peat, Car Owner Craig Lang and Shelby Employees Pat Rogers and Pam Blackwell.

Ken takes a beautiful young lady for the victory lap at Kent.

Ken also decided to run the Drivers' race at Kent. Here, he leads Charlie Hayes's Elva-Porsche (77) and Allen Grant's Cheetah (14) while on his way to a fourth-place finish.

"Player's 200"

On June 6, Ken was back at Mosport in Montreal, Quebec, Canada, for the annual Player's 200, but his luck did not hold. Ken had numerous mechanical problems, which began in practice with a blown engine, and he ended up with another blown engine during the race.

During practice for the Player's 200 at Mosport, Ken points out a problem to Al Dowd as Wally Peat stands by.

At Mosport, Ken leaves no question as to
his choice in the November election. The
car blew up, and he did not finish.

Ken was the ultimate professional and very intense behind the wheel.

Augie Pabst, driving the Shelby-entered King Cobra, gives Ken a ride back to the paddock on the cool-off lap.

Watkins Glen Grand Prix Race Course

Shelby American next focused on the June 28 race at Watkins Glen. Ken and Leslie started Nos. 1 and 2 on the grid for the Manufacturers' race. At the start of the race, Ken and Ed left a bit of room between their two cars, which was filled by Bob Johnson, who darted between the two from the second row. Ken reeled Johnson back in and went on to traverse the 101.2 miles in 64 minutes, 7.2 seconds to secure the win.

USRRC Greenwood

Ken continued his dominant streak on June 19 at Greenwood by winning in GT and placing fourth overall in front of 18,500 fans in Indianola, Iowa.

USRRC Meadowdale

On August 9, Shelby American had cars one state over in Illinois for the eighth race in the USRRC 10-race season. Ken began the weekend by posting the fastest lap in the Manufacturers' trials, lapping the 3.27-mile track in 2:05.2.

Bob Johnson provided some tough competition and raced neck and neck for most of the 120 miles. Both cars came off the Monza wall in unison, virtually drag racing to the checkers with Ken ahead by a car length to win GT.

USRRC Mid-Ohio

After being nipped by Ken at Meadowdale, Johnson was on the giving end of the nipping in GT, finishing 1.2 seconds ahead in the 42-lap race on August 30. Ken was in front when Johnson started drawing him back in, officially passing him for good on the 37th lap.

Road America 500

The Road America 500 on September 13 was not only the final USRRC race of the season but it was also a completely different, very popular, annual, longtime event. The race always had an entry list of 60-plus cars and several well-attended support races. One of those races was The Badger 200, where Ken ran the Shelby Sunbeam Tiger.

At the Road America Badger 300 in September 1964, Ken gets ready to go. The Badger 300 was a support race to the main event, the Road America 500.

He ran well until he was beset with problems that forced him out of the race. In a conversation I had with Ken regarding the Tiger project, Ken told me that the Tiger was basically not a bad car but that the Shelby crew had no time to really develop it due to everything going on in the shop at the time.

In the 500-mile event, Ken was teamed with Ronnie Bucknum in the No. 98 car. Ken put the Shelby Cobra on the third row against many highly modified cars and well ahead of any of the other GT cars. Ken and Bucknum were extremely aggressive in their driving and had to be, given the compe-tition they faced.

Ken and Bucknum were never out of the top five while the car ran and even had the overall lead for a short time. On the 82nd lap, the Cobra that had been driven so hard by the duo was retired. Ken then did a few laps in the No. 97 car but finally stepped into the No. 98 Cobra driven by John Morton and Skip Scott. Ken drove the last 50 laps in an attempt to catch the leader, but he had to settle for second place overall and first in the GT cate-gory. This was Ken's second GT win in two years at Road America.

Ken drove the Shelby Sunbeam Tiger in the Badger 300 and didn't finish due to engine problems.

Ken talks to codriver Ronnie Bucknum before the start of Road America 500 practice.

During the opening lap of the Road America 500, Ken (98) leads Ed Leslie (99), Walt Hansgen's Ferrari 250 LM (2), and Joe Buzzeta's Elva Mk 75 Porsche (79), among others.

Ken cruises along
in the No. 98 Cobra
before having major
problems.

Ken feels the heat after a driver change during the Road America 500.

Ken switched to No. 97 after the No. 98
car blew on Lap 82.

Ken drives to victory lane after finishing second overall and first in the GT class. Along for the ride are codrivers John Morton, Skip Scott, and the crew of Cecil Bowman, Kerry Agapiou, Peyton Cramer, and Pat Rogers who is holding the company mascot, Herman.

Bridgehampton 500

The Bridgehampton 500 was the last FIA points scoring race of the season and was held on September 20. The Shelby team was out to score the maximum number of points and brought every Cobra that was available to race to close the gap on Ferrari, which had already clinched the World Championship for the year.

Ken led the contingent and won the GT race, and the maximum number of points were scored. Shelby American lost the championship by 6.3 points: Ferrari had 84.6, and Shelby American had 78.3.

Ken Miles (98) leads Bill Wonder's Genie-Ford (86) and another entrant at the Bridgehampton 500 in September 1964.

Total concentration is evident here as Ken races to victory at Bridgehampton.

Ken is in victory lane with Shelby next to him and Al Dowd behind him. I always got a wave from Ken.

Los Angeles Times Grand Prix

The Los Angeles Times Grand Prix was one of the greatest sports car races in the world, and it was the race that every driver wanted to win. The annual race in October always drew a huge crowd along with every top team and driver in the world to the hot and often dusty Riverside International Raceway.

Along with the 200-mile grand prix, there was the ever-popular three-hour Enduro support race. Ken was entered in that race in the Shelby Sunbeam Tiger. As always, Ken gave it his best, but the Tiger wasn't up to it and again ran into problems that caused it not to finish.

For the main event, Ken chose to try and qualify his USRRC 289 Cobra for the big race. This was a serious uphill battle considering the competition he was up against. However, against all odds, Ken managed to qualify for the race even though he was well back in the field.

On race day, when the green flag fell, Ken took off in pursuit of the front-runners even though his car was not in their class. Ken drove the car extremely hard and by mid-race, he broke the rear axle coming out of Turn 6, which ended a great effort. Ken told me when we returned to the shop, "I gave it a hell of a go, but we were just totally outclassed."

Ken talks to Shelby American's retired driver Bob Holbert before the start of practice for the Los Angeles Times Grand Prix at Riverside in October 1964. Jack Hoare is behind Ken.

Potent New Powerplant

While these races were taking place, a special lightweight Cobra was being built for Ken Miles. It would be powered by a special experimental, all-aluminum 390-ci engine.

"We built two of those engines for Shelby with the idea that they would eventually replace the well-worn 289-ci engine in the production cars," said Ray Geddes. "In the meantime, one blew up during a dyno test and the other was fitted into the new Miles car that was being built in the shop."

As soon as the car was complete, it was time to take it to Riverside to be tested. The car was originally scheduled to be entered in the upcoming Los Angeles Times Grand Prix at Riverside depending on the test results.

It was cool and rainy that Sunday morning at Riverside. After unloading and getting the car sorted out, it was time to go. After a couple off slow laps, Ken stood on the gas, the front wheels came up, and the car burned rubber all the way to Turn 1.

When Ken came back to the pit area where we were all gathered to hear his opinion, he said, "This thing is ungodly and the fastest thing that I have ever driven, but it needs a lot of work before we run it in competition."

Ken then turned to tire testing with his trusty 289 Cobra.

Back in the shop, Ken served as a judge for one of our periodic engine-lifting contests. The idea was to see who could lift the engine the highest off the shipping pallet. It was all in good fun, and it provided some laughter for the mounting business at hand.

Here is a dyno test of the awesome 390-ci aluminum engine. The sound of that engine running on the dyno was unforgettable.

Ken chose to attempt to qualify
his 289 Cobra for the Grand
Prix because his modified
Cobra was not yet race ready.
And yes, he qualified to run in
the main event.

Miles (98) leads Ronnie Bucknum (5) and Richie Ginther (92), who are driving Shelby King Cobras, out of Riverside's famed Turn 6 during practice for the Los Angeles Times Grand Prix.

Ken Miles started toward the back of a very loaded field and drove extremely hard to move up in the standings.

Ken mixes it up with Tony Settember's Webster 2-Liter (14), Bart Martin's Cooper Ford (187), and John Morton's Lotus 23 (99). None of these cars finished the race.

Ken literally drove the wheels off of his Cobra, and he broke an axle midway through the race while exiting Turn 6.

Nassau Speed Week

When Ken decided to pass on attempting to qualify for the San Francisco Examiner Grand Prix at Laguna Seca a week later, he turned his full attention to the readying of the 390 Cobra for its debut at the annual Nassau Speedweek event on November 29. Also, work was underway on the first Shelby Mustang GT350R at this time, and Ken oversaw and had a hand in the testing of that car too. By the time the 390 Cobra arrived at Nassau, it was ready to get with the program—at least everyone thought so.

The first big event of the week was the Nassau Tourist Trophy, and Ken was entered in the big Cobra. When the green flag fell, Ken immediately shot into the lead, and by the end of the first lap, he had stretched the lead to a quarter-mile. While that car ran, it *really* ran and was easily the fastest car on the track. The problem was that it didn't run well enough for long enough.

On the extremely rough Oakes Field circuit, the suspension started to go, and finally the engine blew. The terrible performance of the two Ford GTs in this race would soon change Ken's life forever.

The big race of the week was the Nassau Trophy Race, and Ken was again entered in the big Cobra. This time, a new 427-ci engine was mounted in the car to replace the blown 390, but again it only lasted 40 laps before it blew up. That was the last time this car was ever run in competition.

Facing Page: By the time Nassau Speed Week approached in late November 1964, the lightweight Cobra was ready for its debut, and what a debut it was. By the end of Lap 1, the car had a quarter-mile lead on the rest of the field.

As the race progressed, the Cobra's suspension and engine began to fail. Soon, it became a two-man race between two of the best drivers of the era: Roger Penske in his Corvette Grand Sport (82) and Ken in the Cobra (98). Bob Johnson's Shelby Cobra (92) and John Cannon's Corvette Grand Sport (00) are in the background.

This is one of the very few color action shots that exists of this car. It shows Ken on the rain-swept Oakes Field circuit. That track was extremely rough and torturous on the Cobra's suspension.

Ken leads Richard Holquist's Abarth-Simca (96) at Nassau. On Ken's Cobra, note the larger hood hole on to get more air to the radiator.

Ken leads A. J. Foyt's Hussein-Dodge (1) during the Nassau Governor's Trophy Race. Foyt hated that car and neither car finished or was ever raced again. The Cobra was used as a test vehicle.

Ford GT

When we returned to Venice, rumors began running through the shop that the Ford GT program was about to be transferred to Shelby American. I received a call to be at the Trans World Airlines (TWA) airfreight area on a wet Sunday morning to photograph the arrival of the first Ford GT to arrive destined for the Shelby shop.

Ray Geddes told me, "We at Ford were appalled by appearance and the performance of the Ford GT at Nassau. That was the last straw in a dreadful season, and we knew that Ford Advanced Vehicles wasn't getting the job done and that something had to be done quickly to save the program. Transferring the program to Shelby was our only possible salvation."

When the trailer carrying the car pulled up in front of the shop, Ken, John Ohlsen, and Frank Lance were there to meet the car. Ken was appalled by the overall condition of the car and couldn't understand how a so-called professional operation could ship a car in that condition internationally. Ohlsen went right to work, giving the car a good steam cleaning. Lance and Ohlsen quickly changed the engine, and the car went to the paint booth for a quick paint job.

"That car was a horrible mess," Ohlsen said. "I had never seen anything like it come into the shop before. Frank and I spent an entire day just getting that car clean enough to bring into the shop. We put one of

The transfer of the Ford GT project to Shelby American in December 1964 began an entirely new chapter in the career of Ken Miles.

When the Ford GTs arrived at the Shelby American shop in late December 1964, they were an absolute mess. A good cleaning, an engine change, and a paint job were all in order. Frank Lance (foreground) and John Ohlsen (in back) work on the engine change.

our engines in that car and sent it across the street to have it painted in our colors."

Lance remembered it this way: "In late December, John Ohlsen and I took over the two Ford GTs that were shipped to us after Nassau. Gordon Chance was assigned to me as my helper, and we had a hell of a lot of work to do to make those cars race ready for Daytona and not much time to do it. We had a lot of changes and modifications to do on those cars to make them race ready, and we also had a lot of testing to do too.

"Ken made huge contributions to this part of the program with ideas and testing feedback. Getting those cars from Nassau junk to winning Daytona less than two months later was one hell of an achievement. While John worked with Ken and Bob on testing, I worked on the Colotti gearboxes that Ford was using at that time for two solid weeks, and with Fords help, we made the last."

The other car arrived a short time later.

When Carroll Smith entered the picture, we were ready to test the first car."

"We were about to go testing with the first car, and, as Ken said, it was a pile of s——," Smith said. "We cut and hacked on those cars until we got them reasonably close to where we wanted them to be for Daytona. Ken and Bob were testing constantly whatever changes we made at Riverside."

The first car was soon packed up and readied for a trip to Riverside for its first testing session.

When Ken arrived at the track, he had his usual morning tea and then took a good look at the car before going out. After a couple of laps, he came in and said, "This car is absolute s——, and I refuse to drive it in this condition."

Bob Bondurant finished the test session.

Ford Executive Leo Beebe said that Ford had finally made the proper decision regarding this project, and he felt that Shelby should have had it from the beginning. Many of us felt the same way.

Once the testing session was over, the real work began, and there was a hell of a lot to do to make those cars ready to race at Daytona on February 28, 1965.

The new car was given a quick paint job and rushed to Riverside in December for its initial test. Phil Remington consults with Ken (seated in car) as John Morton and John Ohlsen look on.

Before going
out, Ken
discusses what
he sees with
John Ohlsen
and Bob
Bondurant.
A young
Peter Miles
is standing
behind his dad.

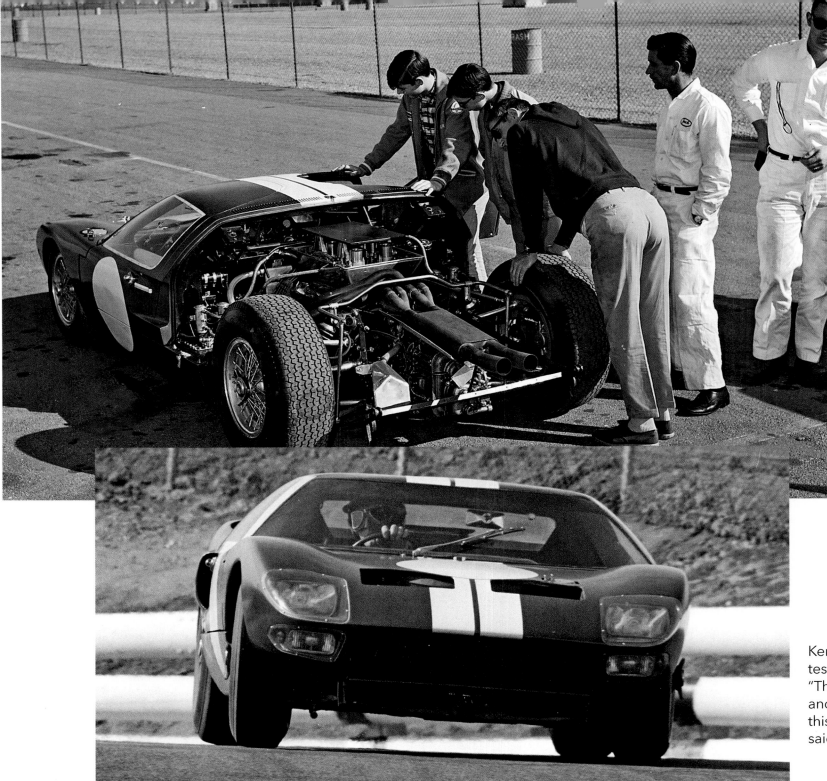

Ken checks the suspension as Peter and a friend look at the car. Crew members Jack Hoare and John Ohlsen are behind Ken.

Ken takes the opening test lap and pulls in. "This car is pure s——, and I won't drive it in this condition," Ken said.

Lloyd Ruby was to be Ken's codriver for the races at Daytona and Sebring. Ruby was a longtime friend and former teammate of Carroll Shelby. Ken and Ruby were an odd couple for sure, but they worked well together. "The first time I ever met or drove with Ken Miles was at Daytona in 1965," Ruby said. "Ken was a high-strung English man, and I was a low-strung Texan. Everyone was wondering how the hell we got together, but it was Carroll who teamed us up. Once we got runnin' together, I really enjoyed being with him. We both liked the same setup on the car and we were both equal. We won several big races together, and Ken was a really great driver. He did a lot of testing on those cars, and that was a big help to me."

Ken Miles was one of the drivers assigned to drive the Ford GT at Daytona and Sebring for Shelby American.

Ken and Shelby talk to another crewmember, likely Carroll Smith, during practice for the Daytona race.

At the beginning of practice,
Ken takes a few slow laps before
really standing on the gas.

Ken sits in his car while waiting to practice as two crew members make adjustments. Charlie Agapiou checks out the progress from the far right.

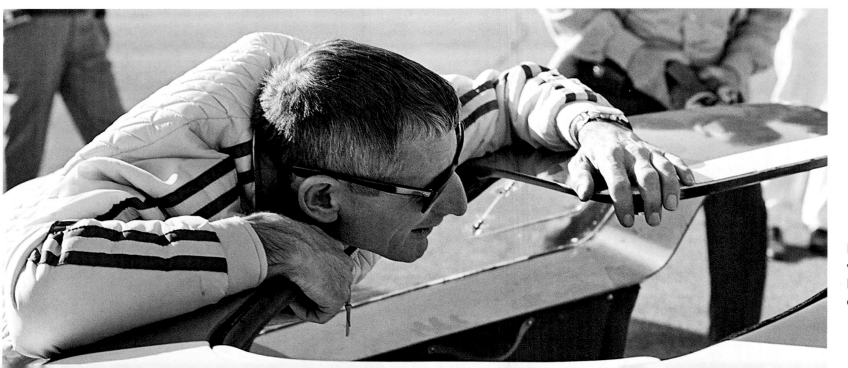

Ken has a word with codriver Lloyd Ruby during practice.

Ken is
auditioning
for my job but
failed the test.

COBRA CREW ONLY

At the end of the day, the to-do list for the Miles/Ruby car was reviewed and taken care of that night.

A great deal of magic happened behind that door, as four Daytona Coupes and two Ford GTs reside inside.

John Ohlsen, Ken's crew chief at this event, takes notes in his book of speed secrets, and he had many.

As the green flag falls, John Surtees's Ferrari 330 P2 (77) takes a brief lead over Bob Bondurant's Ford GT (72), Walt Hansgen's Ferrari 330 (88), Ken's Ford GT (73), and Allen Grant (11), Bob Johnson (12) and Jo Schlesser (13) in Cobra Coupes.

Ken is flat-out at 200-plus mph on the banking at Daytona. With the transfer to Shelby American of these cars, the full potential of this program was beginning to show.

Facing Page: Ken (73) leads the Grant/Leslie (11) Cobra Coupe out of the infield, leading onto the Daytona banking.

Ken (73) leads Dan Gurney's Lotus 19J-Ford (44) down the infield straight. Back in the pack, John Surtees's Ferrari 330 P2 (77) can be seen.

Ken is on the final bend before leaving the infield. In the background is the first Sunbeam Tiger (5) to ever finish a long-distance race.

Ken (far left) is beaming with delight as he exits the car
during a routine pit stop. Crew Chiefs Frank Lance (left)
and John Ohlsen (right) tend to pit duties as Gordon
Chance (left rear) checks the oil.

Frank Lance (right) checks the brakes while Gordon
Chance checks the oil. Jack Hoare and Peyton Cramer
(wearing Cobra shirts) watch from the background.

This is the shot that I wanted and it's the shot I got. The Miles/Ruby car is in for a pit stop, and the driver receives final instructions before returning to the circuit.

Ken (73) leads Bob Bondurant's Shelby Ford GT (72) and the Porsche 904GTS of Ryan, Becker, and Tidwell (6) through the infield.

This shows a cold and very dark night pit stop at Daytona for the Miles/Ruby Ford GT.

This image shows just how dark and dangerous the Daytona pit area was at night during that time. Note crew members wearing headlamps for additional light.

Ken talks to a member of the crew after a night pit stop. Jacque Passino (white jacket) stands behind Ken.

Two of the best test drivers in the world were paired as a team as Sebring. Bruce McLaren (left) and Ken were a great team.

This is one of my favorite Miles images that was shot in the pits during the Sebring event. Phil Remington stands in the background.

The Shelby American team gets race ready
in the very hot and humid hanger at the
old Sebring airport.

Ken is prominent in this iconic image of the 1965 Sebring start. Can you find him? Hint: He is the third from the bottom in the dark helmet.

Ken leads the Shelby entries into the pit area on the morning of the race.

Bruce McLaren's Ford GT (11) leads the Tullius/Gates Triumph Spitfire (66) and the Shaw/Thompson Shelby Cobra (17) through the old Sebring Eases.

Ken races through the night on a very wet and humid track.

The Shelby team pushes Ken into the small, terribly-lit winner's circle at Sebring. The car finished second overall and first in the Prototype Division.

Ken's codriver Bruce McLaren rounds a corner on the old Sebring course. Note the planes parked in the background.

Ken races down the front straight at Sebring.

During the April
Le Mans Trials, Bruce
McLaren sits in the
Shelby Ford GT
as Ken (right) and
Shelby (left) stand by.

427 S/C

Back at the shop, the first real 427-ci racing car was being built, completed, and readied for testing upon Ken's return. Also, the first of only two Mustang GT350Rs to be built at the Venice shop stood ready for testing.

The first and only factory 427 S/C is being completed. Charlie Agapiou works on the car. Ken debuted it in the Prototype race at the Riverside USRRC in May 1965.

The 427 S/C is ready to go testing at Riverside

USRRC Pensacola

The first leg of the 1965 USRRC season was at Corry Field in Pensacola, Florida. Cobras were driven by Tom Payne and Bob Johnson privately. Payne took first place in GT as Miles was testing for Le Mans in April.

USRRC Riverside

Now, it was back for what would be the last two official Cobra team appearances by Ken in the USRRC Series. For the Manufacturers' race at Riverside in early May, there was a field of 21 cars that took the green flag.

In spite of two spins, Ken won the overall and took Crew Chief Mike Donovan on the victory lap, outpacing Scooter Patrick's Porsche 904 by 28 seconds. In the Drivers' race, Ken debuted the first real 427 Cobra. It ran pretty well for 25 laps, but then problems began to occur, and it retired from the race. The car ran as a team car just once more with Ken driving, and that was at a race in Australia later in the year.

Ken is on the gas at the entrance to Riverside's famed Turn 6 in the Manufacturers' race. This class disappeared from the USRRC at the end of the 1965 season.

Ken leads the always-hard-charging
Scooter Patrick Porsche 904 GTS (33)
at Riverside. They finished the race in
this order.

Ken smiles while
holding the
trophy after the
race.

Testing in Michigan

Also during this time, Ken assisted Kar-Kraft in developing an experimental 427-ci-powered Mk II Ford GT. Ken didn't expect much in the beginning. There were various problems with making the engine fit.

"For one thing, the NASCAR oil pans were no damn good, and the engines sucked air and wiped out the bottom ends," Bob Negstad said.

"Well, hell, I know how to solve that puzzle," Ken said. "I've got an idea to put a series of oil pumps together, and it will make a very low package."

So, Ken fiddled around with the oil pan and drive mechanism. Ron Butler was the wrench on the project. So, we got a dry-sump system for the early GT cars. When we finished that modification, the 427 made 480 hp and was lighter than a 350 Chevy and only slightly heavier than a cast-iron Ford 351.

Now, it was on to the Dearborn Test Track, which wasn't a high-speed track. Well, we managed to piss off the track manager by running 160 mph on the straight. He felt that was not safe, so we were asked to leave.

Then, we went to the Michigan Proving Ground in Romeo, Michigan, which was our high-speed banked 5-mile oval test track. For that first outing, we closed the track down and put Ken in the car. He ran three or four laps to become familiar with the setup. We alternated drivers that morning using Tom Payne and Ken for that test.

After lunch, we put Ken back in the car, and it wasn't long before we were lapping at more than 200 mph. That was a track record there, but once again, we drove the track manager crazy with the speeds we were turning. When Ken was asked what he thought of the car, he said, "This is the car I want to drive at Le Mans."

Ken was our best test driver, and his feedback was incredible. When word reached Don Frey about the success of the Romeo test, he said, "I have always liked Ken Miles. His incredible driving talent is consistently great and his on-sight ideas always seem to work."

Le Mans

Next, it was on to Le Mans in June. Once again, Ken was teamed with McLaren in the No. 1 Ford Mk II. In early practice sessions, both Ken and McLaren loved the overall speed, but the handling was a different story.

The Shelby team prepares a surprise for Ferrari, and what a surprise it was while it lasted.

Shelby Press Day

The new facility at Los Angeles International Airport (LAX) had its press and employee open house in early June, and Ken gave rides in the Ford GT roadster to all comers.

Ed Leslie, Lew Spencer, and Ken (left to right) are ready for the official opening of the Shelby Airport Facility in June 1965. The real Shelby American died when the Venice shop was closed.

Ken takes the press for a quick ride in the Ford GT roadster while the employees watch from the sidelines. One can see why the Venice shop had been completely overwhelmed. "When we finally received the keys and moved into the airport facility, we said, 'Wow, look at all this room,'" Bruce Junior said. "So, Ken got into this Cobra and proceeded to run it around the area outside of the blast wall. We had already been told not to do that because it would interfere with the ground-control radar. After blasting up and down the road a few times, I received several phone calls from the LAX guys, who said, 'We are coming over to talk to you guys about this.' They were very nice about it but said that it interfered with the radar and that they couldn't have that, so it needed to stop now. Interference with planes on the ground-control radar was a serious problem."

The three drivers are ready for the press and employee day in June 1965.

No one had ever seen anything like this at Le Mans. These cars were built by Kar-Kraft in Dearborn, Michigan, and prepared by Shelby American. Spoilers and fins would be added for better handling and stability.

The monster awakens, and it was a monster while it ran. "The engine was great, but the transmission failed us when we were miles ahead," Ken said.

The Miles/McLaren car takes to the track for early practice laps with McLaren at the wheel. "With 7 liters and something like 500 safe horsepower strapped in their tails, these new Fords took a bit of taming," McLaren said. "With some aerodynamic trimming and chassis tuning, these cars were potentially the fastest cars ever seen on that circuit."

Bruce and Ken agreed that the aerodynamics were a major concern, and Shelby fabricator Bill Eaton worked to help solve the problem.

"As it turned out, what we needed was what I called 'Chrysler fins' to make the car more stable at high speed, and after a little work, it did just that," Eaton said.

The Ford transmissions were another story. After Ken and Bruce had practiced with the newly modified car, they absolutely loved what they drove.

"Holy s——!" Ken said. "This is the fastest thing I've ever driven by far." Bruce McLaren concurred.

"Once [it was] sorted out, nothing there could come close to staying with that beast," he said.

When the race started, Ken and McLaren's car was near the front of the pack, and by the end of the first lap, it was in the lead. Things went well for a while until the second hour when Ken and Bruce lost first, second, and third gear, and the handwriting was on the wall. During the fourth hour, the gearbox completely failed. The other big Ford's transmission went away after a few more hours. It was about to hit the fan big time at Ford.

Bill Eaton and his bunch worked their magic right here installing the "Chrysler fins."

Carroll looks at the fins and spoiler added by Bill Eaton to the car. Roy Lunn (right, in white shirt) checks the handy work. "I made the fins for the Mk IIs at Le Mans," Eaton said. "The cars had come from Kar-Kraft and had never been run. As it turned out, we needed, what I called 'Chrysler fins' to make the cars more stable at high speed. When Roy Lunn explained what he wanted, we went out in the backside, behind the pits, and cut up these large sheets of aluminum and bent them over in our trailer. They were a fabricated aluminum piece fitted to the body, which was kind of unique at that time. They were indeed run during the race and worked well. Unfortunately, the Ford transmissions didn't work as well."

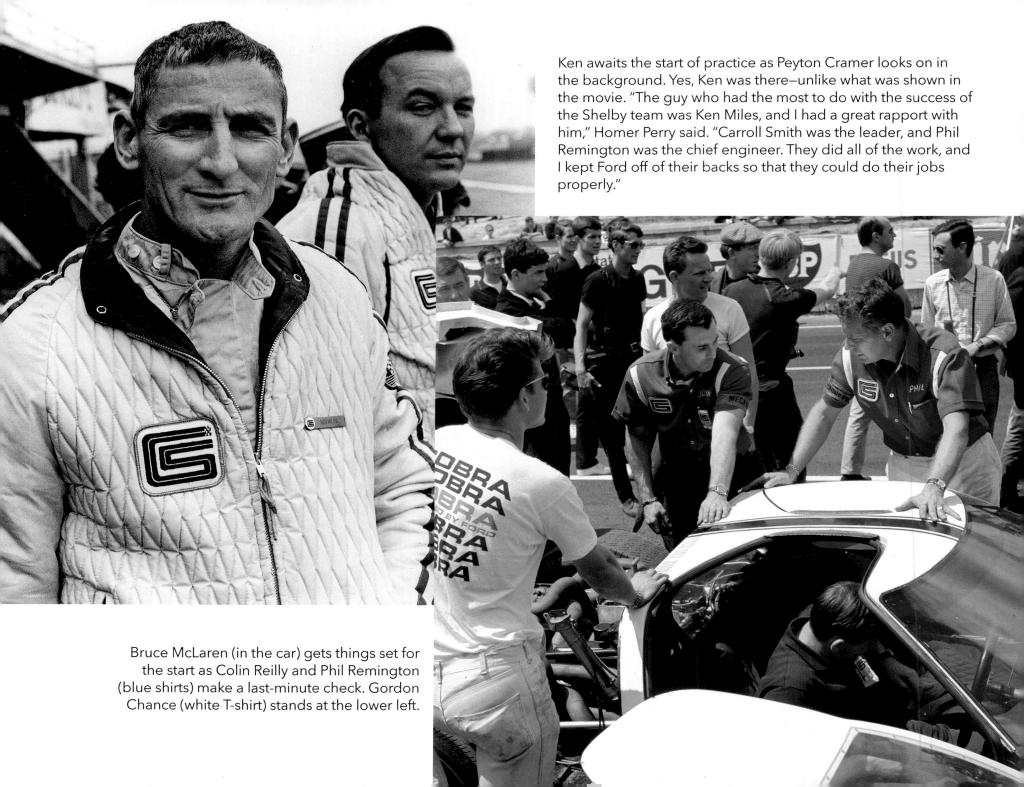

Ken awaits the start of practice as Peyton Cramer looks on in the background. Yes, Ken was there—unlike what was shown in the movie. "The guy who had the most to do with the success of the Shelby team was Ken Miles, and I had a great rapport with him," Homer Perry said. "Carroll Smith was the leader, and Phil Remington was the chief engineer. They did all of the work, and I kept Ford off of their backs so that they could do their jobs properly."

Bruce McLaren (in the car) gets things set for the start as Colin Reilly and Phil Remington (blue shirts) make a last-minute check. Gordon Chance (white T-shirt) stands at the lower left.

Henry Ford II and wife Christina arrive at the circuit. Young Edsel Ford walks behind.

The start of Le Mans was always an exciting event. Chris Amon (2) was very fast off the start, and he was followed by Bob Bondurant (7) and Bruce McLaren (1). McLaren said, "During the first two hours, Chris and I enjoyed some real motor racing in those cars. Chris was first away at the start, but I cruised by as we pulled on to the Mulsanne Straight. We both had to resist the temptation to make those electrifying opening laps a real carve-it-up sprint." Amon said, "I drove one the prototype Mk IIs at Le Mans, and that thing was bloody quick. I had never driven anything like that before. It was an absolute missile."

Bruce McLaren leads Chris Amon at the end of the front straight. No one could stay close to these cars, which just blew away the competition. "If the transmissions would have held up, we would have run [first and second] and won that race by 10 laps," Amon said.

Ken runs away from the field, and the Ferrari's aren't even in sight. "We were in a class by ourselves until the transmissions let go," Ken said. "We broke ours in the fourth hour, and Phil and Chris's lasted until the seventh hour."

"Gearboxes were the Ford jinx in 1964," Bruce McLaren said. "So, in 1965, the two big cars were fitted with special 4-speed monsters made in the USA, and, once again, they broke."

Ken drives at record speeds. Ken said, "Those damn bloody gearboxes cost us that race. This was the fastest car I had ever driven." Bruce McLaren said, "You should have seen all of the finger pointing among the Ford people when things started unraveling. It was almost humorous."

Ken cruises at 200-plus mph, but the gremlins ended up taking hold. "I don't know how many laps we could have won by—probably 10 at least," Ken said.

Two spectators watch the ongoing preparation in the Ford garage at Daytona in February 1966.

in contention. The other Fords fell into their positions according to the prerace plan. All went well for Ken and Ruby, and by the end of the 24-hour race, they were eight laps ahead of second-place Dan Gurney and Jerry Grant when the checkered flag fell.

After the race, Ken said, "That car is a hell of an improvement."

Ruby said, "The Mk II is a really damn good car. It has lots of power, it was very fast, it handled damn good, and Ken and I won our second Daytona race in a row with it."

Ken waits to go out for practice at Daytona. This is one of my favorite images of him.

Ken awaits the start of practice under the watchful eyes of Mike Donovan and Max Kelly (right), and Carroll Smith (left).

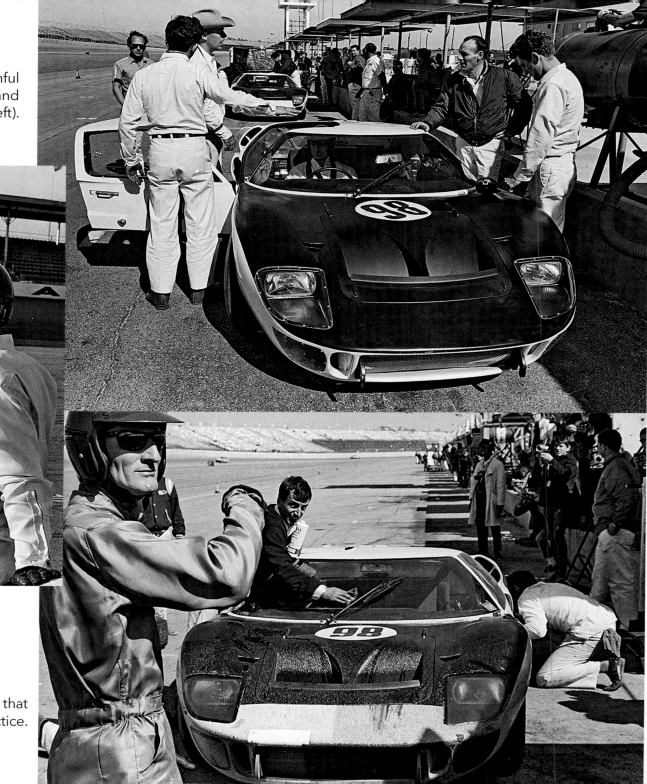

These three were the heart and soul of the Shelby program. Ken, Carroll Smith (left) and Phil Remington (center) go over the Shelby team practice strategy.

Ken tells Lloyd Ruby that it's his turn to practice.

Ken was supremely confident going into the Daytona race. He qualified this car for the pole position at 1:57.0 and was ordered to lead the race at 2:04.0 to 2:05.0. It was felt that this pace would win the race.

Ken leads Mark Donohue (95) and Bruce McLaren (96) out of the infield and onto the high banks during the early part of the race. The Fords were extremely confident at Daytona. "Bill Ines had Sully (Don Sullivan of Ford Engine and Foundry) put the 427 engine together to achieve 500 hp," Shelby said. "They knew reliability was critical, and they achieved that by running four or five complete Le Mans races on the dyno."

Ken's car runs well, and he is in the lead and following Shelby's race plan.

Ken races through the Daytona infield in the afternoon light with the lead.

Ken exits the car during a scheduled pit stop. Lloyd Ruby would take over.

Lloyd Ruby runs at 200-plus mph on the high banks of Daytona. Behind Ruby is the Guldstrand/Wintersteen Penske–entered Corvette that won the GT class.

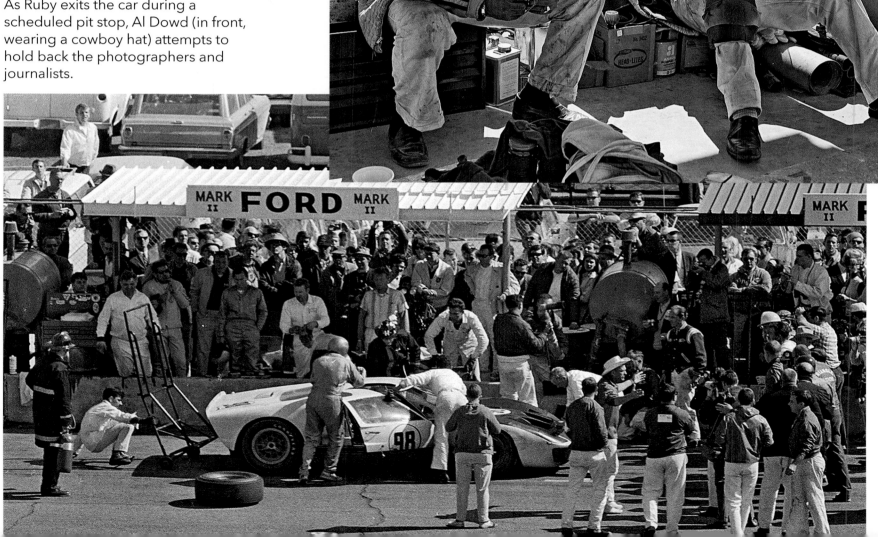

Phil Remington and the Shelby crew show the effects of long-distance racing.

As Ruby exits the car during a scheduled pit stop, Al Dowd (in front, wearing a cowboy hat) attempts to hold back the photographers and journalists.

Ken leads the Bianchi/van Ophem/Beurlys Ferrari 365 P2 (25) in the late afternoon light coming out of the infield onto the high banks.

A night pit stop at Daytona was a real adventure since there was (in this era) very little light in the pit boxes, and it was always cold and very uncomfortable at that time of the year.

Jerry Bondio refuels the Miles/Ruby Ford Mk II late at night. That heavy hose made this job one for a big, strong man.

At one time, you could get on the grass right at the edge of the front straight. Because of the darkness, Ken's pit sign is a lighted box with numbers on it. It was crude, but it worked.

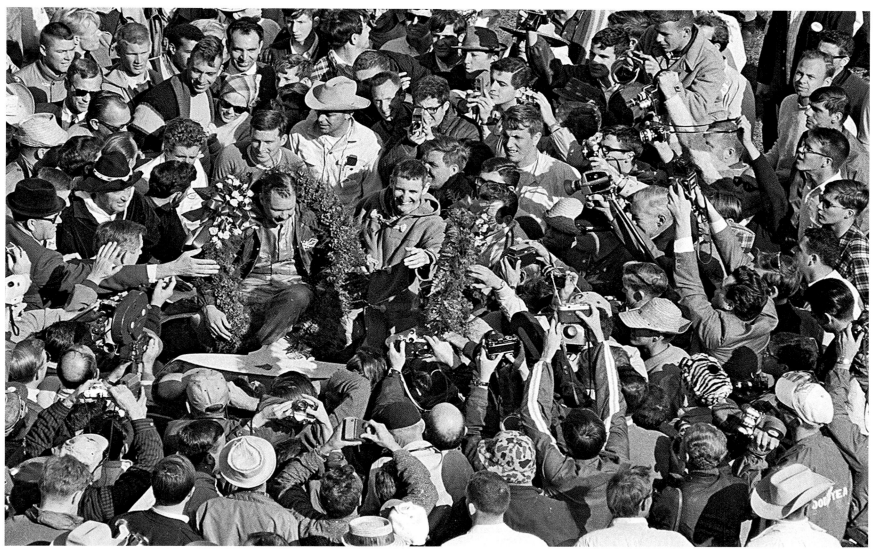

Ruby and Ken are mobbed after winning the race. Carroll, Mike
Donovan, and Charlie Agapiou are visible at the left, and Carroll
Smith and Bill Eaton are just behind Ken.

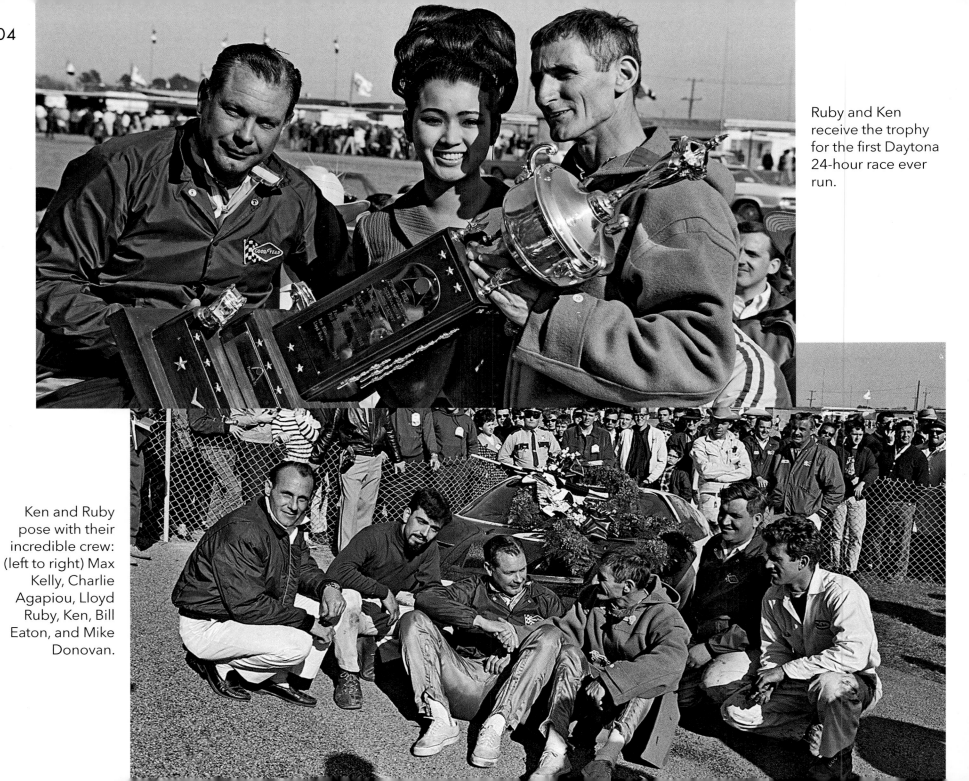

Ruby and Ken receive the trophy for the first Daytona 24-hour race ever run.

Ken and Ruby pose with their incredible crew: (left to right) Max Kelly, Charlie Agapiou, Lloyd Ruby, Ken, Bill Eaton, and Mike Donovan.

12 Hours of Sebring

Now, it was onto Sebring to see if the lightweight roadster X1 project that Bob Negstad and Ken spent so much time working on during the winter would really live up to expectations.

After the X1 was shipped from Kar-Kraft to Shelby American, the car was completely rebuilt. The chassis structure was completely rebuilt to Shelby American specs, a rollover bar was fabricated and installed, the short nose and all substructure was mounted, and a coupe tail was fitted to utilize the proven oil cooler, rear brake, and carburetor air ducting.

Practice went well, despite two broken automatic transmissions and a switch back to a manual transmission. Despite those problems, Ken and Ruby were pleased with the car's overall practice performance.

Ken was asked to not qualify quickly; therefore, the car started in fifth position. Ken and Ruby were told before the race to lap at 3:01, stay within striking distance of the leaders, and never run in lower than third place.

Orders also included breaking the Ferrari and staying close to Gurney.

The race went well and according to plan. Although, Ken's car had a late race change of front brake rotors. Ken's hunch that Gurney was punishing the engine was proven to be correct, as Gurney's Mk II sputtered to a stop on Lap 227 due to a failure. Gurney pushed the car across the finish line but was disqualified for doing so.

In winning the race, Miles and Ruby set a new Sebring race record, covering 1,286 miles at an average speed of 98.6 mph. In victory lane, Ken said, "The car was fantastic. It was a great day for Ford, but I'm ashamed to win this way. I feel sorry for Dan [Gurney]. He deserved to win, as he was magnificent."

Ruby said, "We really lucked into the win here. I was in the shower when I found out that I had to go to victory lane. What a shock that was. I guess you never know what's going to happen in the final laps. Gurney and them guys were supposed it win that race, and they should have. We really lucked out on that one."

The Shelby hanger at Sebring was a very busy place.

This is another view of Shelby American's busy hanger. Those hangers were very hot and humid.

Ken's crew checks the last-minute details closely. "At Daytona, Gurney thought that Ken had a better crew, so at Sebring we switched crews," Charlie Agapiou said. "As fate would have it, Ken won anyway."

Steele Therkleson, Phil Remington, and Ken Miles work to change another transmission on the X1 roadster. This was one of the several transmission changes made during practice.

The crew of the Miles/Ruby roadster poses for a prerace photo. Ron Butler, Eric Leighton, and Colin Riley look ready to go.

The start of the 1966 12 Hours of Sebring shows Ken (fifth from the bottom in the dark helmet) running toward his car.

The Miles/Ruby Mk II roadster was not asked to qualify quickly; therefore, this car started in fifth position. Numerous changes had been made after the car was received by Shelby American from McLaren through Kar-Kraft. The chassis was completely rebuilt to Shelby American specs. The chassis structure was strengthened at the rear hoop joint, crash damage was repaired, a rollover bar was fabricated and installed, and the short nose and substructure were mounted. A coupe tail was fitted to utilize the proven oil cooler, rear brake, and carburetor air ducting.

Ken was instructed to lap at 3:01.0 and stay within striking distance of the leaders. This car never ran lower than third in the standings. "Ken felt that, in spite of Dan's outstanding performance, he would not finish the race," Charlie Agapiou said. "He told me that Dan's car was pulling him out of the corners despite the fact that Dan's car was heavier than the roadster. Ken felt that this indicated punishment of the engine."

Lloyd Ruby battles the Mike Parkes Ferrari 330 P3 (26) for second place. Ken and Ruby were told to run with the Ferrari and alternate positions. They ran in second and third positions until the Ferrari broke early in the 12th hour.

Ken follows Shelby's plan and laps consistently while saving the car.

Ken exits the car during a scheduled pit stop while Charlie Agapiou runs to retrieve a brake part.

Lloyd Ruby waits for his turn at the wheel. Ruby was a great guy and a fast one too.

Ruby goes around the old Webster Turns according to plan.

Charlie Agapiou is busy changing the brake rotors on the Miles/Ruby car.

Chris Economaki interviews Ken and Lloyd Ruby in victory lane for the second time in two years.

Because of the extremely dark pits, this is maybe one of the only color images that exists of Ken leaving the pits near the end of the race.

Dan Gurney (2) pushes his Ford Mk II into the pits after he had pushed the car across the finish line only to be disqualified.

Ken heads up the old Sebring straight.

The roadster makes a pit stop, and Ken re-enters the car as the race moves toward its conclusion.

LE MANS PROGRESS MEETING NO. 9

SEBRING RACE   (March 26)

The first place X-1 Roadster set a new Sebring Race record, covering 1286 miles at an average speed of 98.6 mph. The Mark II driven by Gurney, which led most of the race, failed a rod bolt on the last lap but would have finished second had he not pushed his car and been disqualified. The second place Mark II was a Holman & Moody entry, followed by a production GT 40 which finished third. The only other Mark II, which was an automatic, finished in twelfth position.

Both Alan Mann Mark I (289 CID) entries dropped out due to a slipping clutch in one car and broken valve springs in the second. Neither car had sufficient power to be competitive with the Mark II's, even with the reduced weight and handling modifications.

The brake problems experienced on the Alan Mann and Holman & Moody entries were primarily due to excessive driver usage, which resulted in an abnormal deflection or dishing of the rotors.

The Shelby American prepared Mark II driven by Dan Gurney completed the entire race without incident and required no rotor change. On the winning car, a crack became evident to the driver after nearly 10 hours and required a change of front rotors.

A page from the Ford Race Report tells the story.

Practice for Le Mans

Le Mans practice came soon after the race at Sebring concluded, and Ken was one of several drivers involved in the wet testing sessions in France. When Ken's turn came, he spun at the Indianapolis turn at approximately the same time as the Walt Hansgen accident, losing a Gilmer belt off the Shelby's dry-sump oil system. However, no other damage was incurred. Ken's testing time was pretty well finished after that due to the testing time constraints.

Once back at Shelby American, Ken was off to Riverside for development tests to finalize the braking system to be used at Le Mans. Ken tested new brake rotors, pistons, and seals for the new brakes. It should also be noted that he did some engine testing at the same time.

By the time the teams were ready to depart for Le Mans in June, Ford was gearing up in a way that had never been seen before for the upcoming race. No expense was spared, and the three Shelby cars were only the tip of the iceberg.

Ken was one of several drivers who drove this car at the Le Mans trial in April. He drove very few laps but had a spin at Indianapolis on the circuit. Carroll Smith talks to one of the drivers as Sherman Falconer stands by.

Ken and Carroll stand in front of a Ford Mk II driven by Ken at the Le Mans trials in April. Some of the Shelby crew fall in behind for the photo: (left to right) Bill Eaton, Sherman Falconer, Charlie Agapiou, Carroll Smith, Ron Butler, Jerry Bondio, Gary Kioke, Al Dowd, and Phil Remington line up behind.

The cars are ready for shipment to Le Mans.

LE MANS PRACTICE (Cont'd.)

suffered injuries which proved fatal. The estimated speed of the vehicle was 100 to 130 mph.

Ken Miles spun at the Indianapolis turn at approximately the same time as the Hansgen accident, losing a Gilmer belt off the Shelby dry sump oil system, but incurring no other damage.

Practice continued in the afternoon with the J-Car for initial shakedown and aerodynamic stability.

SUNDAY (April 3)

The track was dry with overcast skies and an ambient temperature between 45 - 60°F.

Suspension, brake, and engine data was recorded on both the Mark II and the J-Car at 3:36 to 3:38 lap times. A peak brake temperature of 1250°F. indicates a much less severe braking condition than Sebring and substantiating our previous theory that Le Mans is much easier on brakes than most circuits. The suspension showed no excessive lift due to high speed aerodynamics. A 2:77 over-all axle ratio in the Mark II and a 2:58 in the J-Car gave engine RPM's of 6200 and 6400 respectively. The fastest time for the practice was a 3:34.4 in the J-Car, followed by a 3:36 in the Mark II.

The two Alan Mann (289 CID) cars turned times of 3:38 and 3:40; however all these drivers, when given a ride in the Mark II, preferred the 427 CID engine over the 289 CID. All Le Mans entries will be powered by the 427 CID engine.

This Ford report page notes Ken's spin.

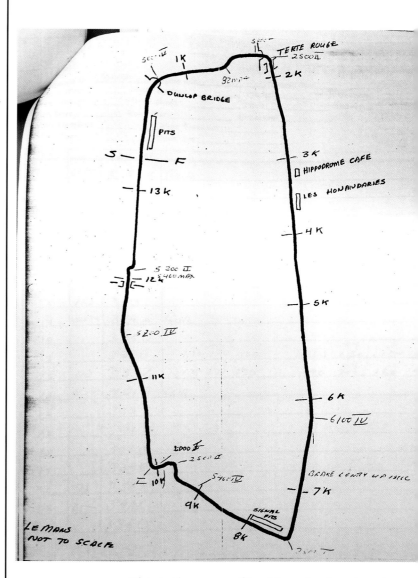

This is the map of Le Mans (as it existed then) that was provided to all of the Shelby drivers before practice began.

The Peugeot Garage in Le Mans was home to the Ford team in 1966, and it was a very busy place.

Charlie Agapiou and his crew were very involved with their car's preparation. John Collins bends over the front end of the car.

Dan Gurney (3) leads Ken Miles (1) out of the Mulsanne hairpin. Gurney was told to lap at a pace consistent with both finishing and breaking the Ferraris. Gurney was also told to lap at 3:37.0 to 3.38.0 to save the engine, save the brakes, and lead the race. Ken was to run second about 1 to 2 seconds behind Gurney. "There was some talk in the pits that Ken did not follow team orders and pushed Gurney to the point of breaking," Charlie Agapiou said. "That was absolute bulls——. Ken followed his directions to the letter. When he pitted on Lap 1 to fix the door, Ken lost several places. After returning to the race, he had to go like hell to get back in second place behind Dan. That's where he was told to be."

Ken rounds the Dunlop curve as hundreds of thousands watch. "You could never discount the Ferraris," Ken said. "They were down on power, but they were much deeper in racing experience then we were, and the talent of their drivers was superb."

Ken is deep in thought as he prepares to re-enter his car.

Ken rounds the Mulsanne Hairpin. "Driving into the late afternoon or early morning sun is a bloody nuisance," Ken said. "You can't see anything; it absolutely blinds you."

During a scheduled pit stop, Denny Hulme exits the car as Ken stands by to take over.

As Gurney's car undergoes repairs in the foreground, Ken exits the pits.

VOITURES	1	2	3	4	5	6	7	8	9
TOURS	211	210	210	12	204	97	110	30	

VOITURES	32	33	34	35	36		38		
TOURS	193	193	110	166	14		0		

S.E

The Le Mans scoreboard shows that Ken was indeed a lap ahead— as we all knew he was.

Ken prepares to re-enter the car as Derek Eaton offers a quick word of encouragement.

Ken enters the car as Crew Chief Charlie Agapiou (right) holds the door.

Ken races down the front straight at Le Mans, following team orders and staying out of trouble.

Leo Beebe was the head of Ford Racing and had to make some very tough decisions, but he was not the idiot portrayed in the *Ford v Ferrari* movie. There was obviously no research by the writer of that dreadful script. "When Henry Ford II saw me at the starting line before the race, he handed me a card that said 'You better win, HFII,'" Beebe said.

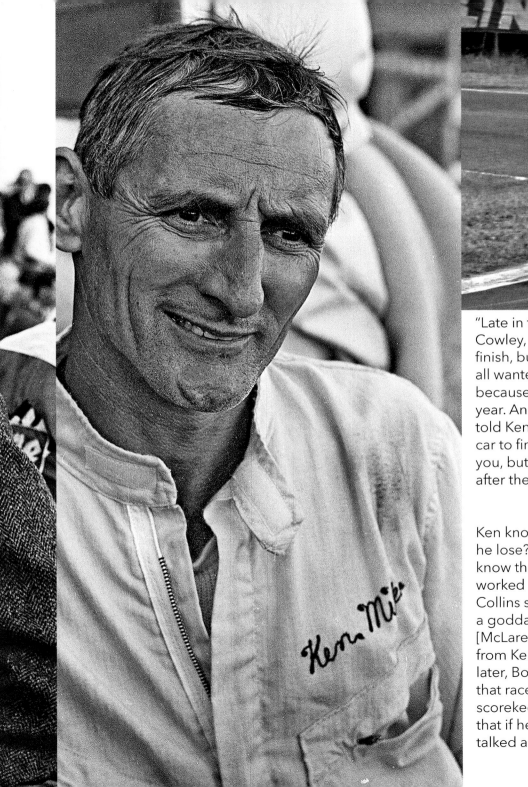

"Late in the race when I saw Beebe, [Jacque] Passino, and his stooge, [John] Cowley, huddled together I could tell that something was up regarding the finish, but I wasn't advised of what that decision was," Carroll Smith said. "We all wanted Ken to win Le Mans after his successes at Daytona and Sebring because he would have been the first to win all three of those races in one year. And we knew he was a lap ahead at that time. I don't know what they told Ken during that final pit stop, but he wasn't very happy as he entered the car to finish the race. I leaned over and told him, 'I don't know what they told you, but you won't be fired for winning Le Mans.' He would never talk about it after the race was over, and we were the best of friends."

Ken knows that something is up to steal the race away from him. How could he lose? He was a lap ahead, and his car was running strong. Little did he know that Passino and Cowley were plotting to take a lap away from him. "I worked with Charlie Agapiou on Ken Miles's car at Le Mans in 1966," John Collins said. "I know that we were a lap in the lead at the finish; Ken had to be a goddamn lap in the lead because he was running a lot quicker than Bruce [McLaren] at the time. That whole finish was bull––, and Ford stole that race from Ken. How can you run quicker and finish up behind the guy?" Years later, Bob Negstad, who was an engineer at Kar-Kraft, told me that Ken won that race. "Ken was indeed a lap ahead when Ford sent me to the French scorekeepers to have a lap taken away," Negstad said. Negstad was told that if he ever said anything about that incident, he would be fired. He never talked about it until he retired from Ford.

The final stop for the Miles/Hulme Ford finds Carroll Shelby (far right) telling Ken and Denny Hulme of the decision to have a blanket finish. "After Carroll talked to Ken during the final pit stop, I heard Ken say, in a loud voice, 'So ends my f——ing contribution to this bloody motor race,' and he threw his sunglasses across the pit," John Collins said.

Ken and Charlie Agapiou, a longtime friend and the crew chief, confer during a late race pit stop. "Ford didn't want Ken to win at Le Mans," Agapiou said. "They wanted the headlines to read 'Ford Wins Le Mans,' not 'Miles becomes the first to Sweep Daytona, Sebring, and Le Mans.' Ken told me that in spite of any Ford decision, he wasn't going to finish second."

The arranged blanket finish obviously didn't happen as planned. Bruce McLaren leads Ken Miles and Dick Hutcherson across the finish line in one of the most controversial and fouled-up finishes in the history of Le Mans. "I wanted Ford to win," Leo Beebe said. "We called Ken in and slowed him down so that Bruce and Chris would win. I think that they deserved to win. They ran a good race and did what we had told them to do."

Facing Page: Phil Remington talks to a very distraught Ken Miles as a less-than-happy Bruce McLaren (foreground) contemplates the Ford-ordered blanket finish. "I guess that 1966 will always be remembered for the huge controversy that was created by the arranged finish," said Jacque Passino. "As you remember, we had three cars running up at the front as the race was drawing to its conclusion. Ken Miles was in one, and Dick Hutcherson and Bruce McLaren were in the others. All of those guys were real racers. Miles would race his grandmother to the breakfast table, and the other two weren't much better. We figured that in order to ensure a Ford win and keep those three guys from racing each other to the end, that we would have a dead-heat finish. We didn't want to risk those guys crashing each other or breaking the cars. In hindsight, we probably should have done it differently, but we were trying to control our destiny and ensure a Ford win, and we did just that."

Ken Miles heads for the victory stand with Denny Hume sitting on the decklid waving to the crowd. Who had won? "We thought we had won, and when we attempted to push the car to the victory stand, the French officials stopped us and said that we didn't belong there—that we'd finished second," Charlie Agapiou said. "Ken was sitting in the car and said to me, 'I think I've been f——ed.' We were all under the distinct impression that despite the finish, we were a lap ahead at the end."

So close, yet so far. The Miles/Hulme Ford Mk II sits abandoned at the finish line as the victory celebration continues in the background. "At Le Mans, I was the guy who Jacque Passino sent over to Ken Miles to tell him to back off and let the other guys catch up," Bob Negstad said. "Ken got tears in his eyes and said, 'No, this is my only opportunity to do this, and I can't do that and I won't do that.' During the next pit stop, Ken's codriver was told to slow down and let the others catch up, and Denny did as he was told. It was during this time that Passino sent John Cowley down to the scorer and timer's tower and told them that we had mis-credited a lap on Ken's car and to take a lap away from that car. When the car came in for its final stop, Ken got back into the car and refused to participate in the prescribed finish. That's why he laid back when the three cars crossed the finish line. Ken was a lap ahead at the finish. That's true. That's absolutely, totally true. He was a lap ahead, and Passino and Cowley went down and took the lap away. They absolutely stole that race from Ken, and it's about time that the truth is told. Ken's memory deserves that. When this quotation was shown to Carroll Smith, he said, "Bob Negstad is one of the most truthful people that I have ever known." Negstad died shortly after this interview was conducted, and many of us feel that it was a dying declaration to see justice finally done for his good friend, Ken Miles.

Although in this case it was felt that the violence of the crash would have caused fatal injuries no matter how strong the chassis structure had been, the complete disintegration of the cockpit area and the sheer failure of the front chassis section (as compared to the excellent chassis structure behavior in previous Ford GT and Ford Mk II high-speed crashes) was apparent. This indicates that aluminum honeycomb is not a suitable material for structural use in a heavy high-speed racing car.

Carroll Smith was there.

"That was the saddest and worst day of my life," Smith said. "When I was finally able to call Carroll [Shelby] and tell him what happened, there was complete silence. You could hear two grown men crying that day. It was on the last lap of the last testing day in the last corner. Why?"

Carroll Shelby remembered receiving Smith's call.

"When Carroll Smith called me in the late afternoon of that terrible day crying, I knew that something very serious had happened," he said. "When I heard the news, I went into complete shock. I began to cry, as I knew how much Ken had meant to me personally and to Shelby American as a company. As you know, I hadn't cried since Dave MacDonald's funeral in 1964."

Homer Perry was there too.

"Complete shock," Perry said. "I couldn't comprehend it until I sat down. I loved Ken, as he was a great guy and did so much for our program."

Ken's son, Peter, was 15 years old when he saw it happen.

"I was up by the administration building in a rental car, practicing my driving," Peter said. "I could hear the race car, but it suddenly got quiet. I looked down toward Turn 9, and I could see a ball of flame flying through the air.

"I got to the scene as fast as I could, but everyone else was ahead of me. Since the car was burning, I asked, 'Can't we just put it out and get my father out of the car?'

"Carroll Smith said that he was not in the car. So, I asked where he was because I expected to see him walking around. Carroll pointed to where he was lying in the dirt.

"He was lying in the dirt with his right leg bent back at the knee so his foot was closer to his head. I started to go over there, but Carroll said, 'Don't go.' I could tell that he was more damaged than just his knee, but I couldn't see any other details other than his helmet next to him with the chin strap still done up.

"Carroll and I drove around the track looking for a possible clue as to the cause, but we saw nothing until we got to Turn 9, where we saw two skid marks leave the track and go over the embankment," Peter continued. "So, my conclusion was that there was either a brake failure or the driveline locked up. Otherwise, there would have been four marks.

"That was really hell for me to go through, and it scarred me for a long, long time. People didn't get grief counseling in those days. I've seen the movie five times, and I cry every time I see it."

Bob Negstad was not there but had spent a lot of time with Ken at the races and at testing.

"When I heard that horrible news, I went into complete shock," Negstad said. "I had to sit down before I fell down. Ken was the backbone of our program and impossible to replace. I was in tears and still am when I think about it. I really loved that guy; he was our program."

Charlie Agapiou wasn't there, but he was Ken's longtime crew chief and good friend.

"On August 10, 1966, I was drafted into the Army, and Ken was killed at Riverside on August 17, 1966, which was my birthday. What a horrible day that was," Agapiou said. "I often wonder if I'd been at Riverside that day, could I have somehow prevented that accident from happening? Of course, I'll never know."

In a recent interview, I asked Agapiou that very question. His answer was, "No."

This may be the only photograph of the engine/automatic transmission combination that was being tested by Ken on that fatal day at Riverside.

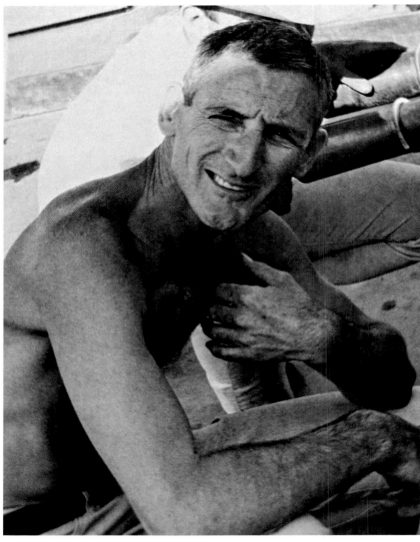

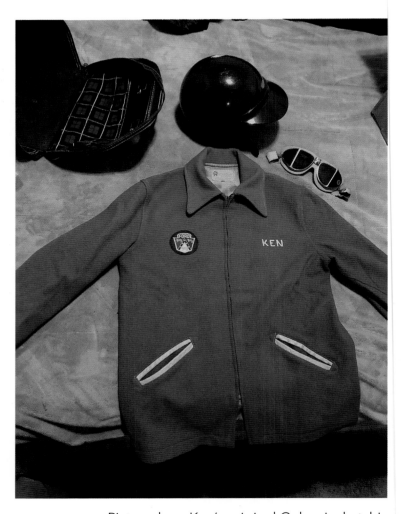

Pictured are Ken's original Cobra jacket, his helmet, goggles, and carrying bag. (Photo Courtesy Peter Miles)

Steele Therkleson contends that this was the last known photo ever taken of Ken alive. This photo was taken about 5 minutes before he went out his final laps. "Everybody who was there has their own version of what happened, but I don't believe that there was ever a concrete finding," Bill Eaton said. "That car was run very hard during the three days of testing, and Ken had driven it exceptionally hard. I'd been dispatched back to L.A. to pick up a new tail section, and I arrived back at Riverside earlier than expected. We never had time to put the new tail on because we just ran out of time. The accident happened on the last lap of the last run of the last day of testing."

SHELEY AMERICAN INC - ENGINEERING & DEVELOPMENT REPORT

Date: 8-15 thru 8-17-66   Track: Riverside Raceway, Riverside, California
Report No: SAI-

PURPOSE: 1. To determine suitability of Ford "J" car for modified sports car
competition.
2. To compare performance of power shift automatic, "jump box",
automatic and type 44 manual transaxles and to evaluate the experimental T&C
torque converter.
3. To determine suitability of Lubrizol 1044 automatic transmission
oil as a "common" lubricant for converter, jump box, ring and pinion and differential.
4. To test the 427 CID race engine equipped with Weber carburetors and
310 camshaft, and with 8V manifold and 310 camshaft.
5. To test cooling package of "J" car.
6. To determine optimum chassis settings for "J" car.
7. To compare Goodyear and Firestone tire performance and wheel
sizes.

VEHICLES:

Ford "J" Car -- Chassis No. J2

DRIVERS:

Ken Miles

PERSONNEL:

Phil Remington   )   Homer Perry - Ford Division
Carroll Smith   )   Dick Byers - T&C
Colin Riley   ) SAI   Joe Calcagno - T&C
John Collins   )   Jim Gates - Instrumentation
Steele Therkelson   )   Anthony Goodlesky - Instrumentation
Derek Eaton   )

- 3a -

COMMENT: (Cont'd)

The ring and pinion were inspected for wear and found satisfactory.
Chassis, steering and engine mounts were inspected and found
satisfactory.

8/17..... 45 laps of the 3.2 mile circuit were run. Fastest lap was 1:52.1.
Arrival of suspension springs allowed suspension adjustments to be
carried out. Spring rates, toe-in and camber, adjustments were
carried out. Road holding was greatly improved.

Preliminary comparison of Goodyear and Firestone tires was conducted.
Wheels with low profile Firestone tires were mounted. At the end
of lap #45, at the beginning of the braking area for turn #9, the vehicle
went out of control, left the road to the right at about the 250 marker;
dropped approximately 10 feet into the infield. The vehicle apparently
landed on its left rear wheel, broke up on impact and burst into flame.

The chassis unit broke in two at the front wishbone attachment substructure. The front suspension wheels, steering and pedals came to
rest against the crash wall about 1/3 of the way through turn #9.

The major part of the vehicle comprising rear suspension, engine,
transaxle, and the rear part of the cockpit came to rest just off the inside
of the track about 1/3 of the way through turn #9.

The driver was thrown clear of the major portion of the vehicle at final
impact and was found about 15 feet ahead of the vehicle. Death was
instantaneous.

Cause of the accident has not been determined. After investigation,
a separate report will be submitted.

******

The front page of the Shelby Test Report lists those present for that terrible day at Riverside.

Page 3A tells what happened. This was a very sad and tragic moment for all of us who knew and worked with Ken Miles at Shelby American from 1963 to 1966.

Safety Improvements

After Ken was killed, Ford upgraded its safety program. Bill Holbrook was in charge of the program.

"I was the one who conducted the crash test on the Ford Mk II," Holbrook said. "This was done shortly after Ken Miles was killed. It was after that accident that we got on a real safety kick regarding our race cars.

"We wanted to hit the wall at 60 mph during the test, but we were hampered by all of the cords and cables. At that time, we had to tow the car because we did not have remote control. As it was, we hit the wall at 51 mph, which was, I think, the fastest crash test that we had ever done at that time. I wish we'd had today's technology. Then, we would have had no problem on achieving the speed we originally wanted.

"After that test, we found that when the rocker panels were crushed, the pressure would go right up the filler neck and blow the fuel lid off. With the front end crushed, it directed the fuel up and over the entire vehicle and caused a very serious fire problem.

"We used Stoddard Solvent to duplicate fuel in this test because its weight closely matches gasoline. Because of this test, a lot of changes were made. The biggest ones were the addition of fuel-cell bladders to prevent fire [as well as] a stronger roll cage. We also did a lot of work in the safety belts. We found that a lot of attaching hardware that was made out of cold-rolled steel broke and bent under stress, so I [now] make stainless-steel fittings. We also added crotch straps and foam backing on the belts.

"I don't know what happened to what was left of that chassis. I can tell you it was history because it was completely crushed. We really learned a lot from all of that testing."

KEN MILES

EPILOGUE: MY FRIEND KEN MILES

When I first met Ken Miles in mid-1958 at Riverside, I instantly liked him. He had a caustic sense of humor that I understood because I grew up around it. But it wasn't until Ken came to us at Shelby American that I really got to know and appreciate him.

Not only was Ken a great driver but he was also a real take-charge guy and problem solver. When he ran our race shop in Venice, there was no bulls——, just hard work. But he did allow for good times to happen, and they did happen often. On his occasional visits to my terribly smelly and unventilated darkroom, he would always ask, "How the hell do you do what you do in this tiny, dreadful place?" I would just laugh and say, "I just make it work."

I will always remember with great fondness, our late evening chats in his office while gluing up those awful homologation papers. His love of classical music filled the room and offered a bit of well-deserved downtime.

I will always remember Ken Miles for all of the advice he gave me and his unbelievable contributions to the Shelby American program.

When Huub Linnenbank, a Dutch gentleman, offered me the usage of his painting for my book, I said, "Why not?" (Painting by Huub Linnenbank; Reproduced with Permission)

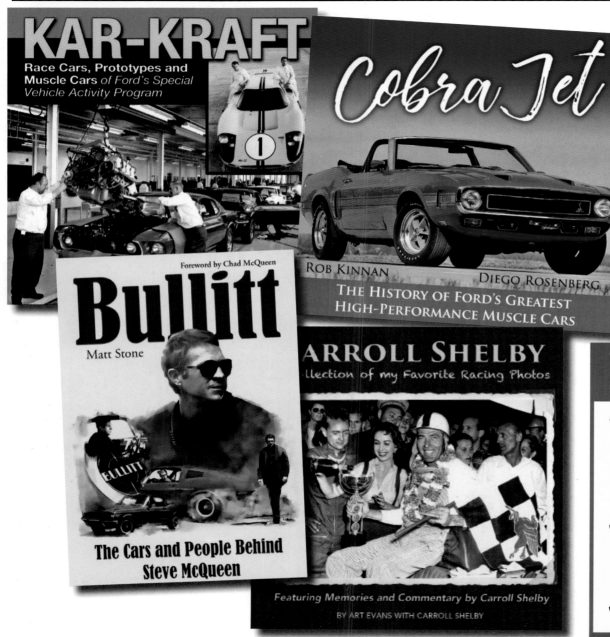